Accounting for Derivatives and Hedges

Steven M. Bragg

AccountingTools®

ISBN 978-1-64221-320-1

For more information about AccountingTools® products, visit our Web site at www.accountingtools.com.

Table of Contents

About the Author

Steven Bragg, CPA, has been the chief financial officer or controller of four companies, as well as a consulting manager at Ernst & Young. He received a master's degree in finance from Bentley College, an MBA from Babson College, and a Bachelor's degree in Economics from the University of Maine. He has been a two-time president of the Colorado Mountain Club, and is an avid alpine skier, mountain biker, and certified master diver. Mr. Bragg resides in Centennial, Colorado. He has written more than 300 books and courses, including *New Controller Guidebook*, *GAAP Guidebook*, and *Payroll Management*.

Steven maintains the accountingtools.com web site, which contains continuing professional education courses, the Accounting Best Practices podcast, and thousands of articles on accounting subjects.

Chapter 1
Derivatives and Hedging Transactions

Introduction

A derivative is a specialized financial instrument that can be used to mitigate risk and engage in speculation. The typical business is more interested in risk mitigation, so in this chapter we focus on the concepts of risk, hedging to ameliorate risk, and the types of derivative hedging tools available – with a specific emphasis on risk reduction related to foreign exchange and interest rates.

What is a Derivative?

A *financial instrument* is a document that has monetary value or which establishes an obligation to pay. Examples of financial instruments are cash, foreign currencies, accounts receivable, loans, bonds, equity securities, and accounts payable. A *derivative* is a financial instrument that has the following characteristics:

- It is a financial instrument or a contract that requires either a small or no initial investment;
- There is at least one *notional amount* (the face value of a financial instrument, which is used to make calculations based on that amount) or payment provision;
- It can be settled *net*, which is a payment that reflects the net difference between the ending positions of the two parties; and
- Its value changes in relation to a change in an *underlying*, which is a variable, such as an interest rate, exchange rate, credit rating, or commodity price, that is used to determine the settlement of a derivative instrument. The value of a derivative can even change in conjunction with the weather.

Examples of derivatives include the following:

- *Call option*. An agreement that gives the holder the right, but not the obligation, to *buy* shares, bonds, commodities, or other assets at a pre-determined price within a pre-defined time period.
- *Put option*. An agreement that gives the holder the right, but not the obligation, to *sell* shares, bonds, commodities, or other assets at a pre-determined price within a pre-defined time period.
- *Forward*. An agreement to buy or sell an asset at a pre-determined price as of a future date. This is a highly customizable derivative, which is not traded on an exchange.

- *Futures*. An agreement to buy or sell an asset at a pre-determined price as of a future date. This is a standardized agreement, so that they can be more easily traded on a futures exchange.
- *Swap*. An agreement to exchange one security for another, with the intent of altering the security terms to which each party individually is subjected.

In essence, a derivative constitutes a bet that something will increase or decrease. A derivative can be used in two ways. Either it is a tool for avoiding risk, or it is used to speculate. In the latter case, an entity accepts risk in order to possibly earn above-average profits. Speculation using derivatives can be extremely risky, since a large adverse movement in an underlying could trigger a massive liability for the holder of a derivative.

When entering into a derivative arrangement, neither party to the arrangement pays the entire value of the instrument up front. Instead, the net difference between the obligations of the two parties is tracked over time, with final settlement being based on the net difference between the final positions of the parties when the instrument is terminated. Also, there is no delivery or receipt of any non-financial item. This arrangement is referred to as *net settlement*.

By minimizing the need for an up-front investment, a business or individual can enter into a derivative arrangement at minimal cost. This makes the use of derivatives much more cost-effective than would be the case if they were paid for up front and in full.

The value of a derivative changes in concert with the variability of the underlying on which it is based. For example, if a derivative is tied to a benchmark interest rate and there is a minimal expectation that the interest rate will change during the life of the derivative, then the seller of the derivative bears little risk of having to pay out, and so will accept a low price for the derivative. Conversely, if there is an expectation of major changes in the underlying, the risk that the seller will have to pay out increases, so the seller will require a much higher price for the derivative.

It is possible for a derivative to not be a financial instrument. In this situation, the terms of the derivative must allow for the option to have a net settlement. Also, it cannot be part of the normal usage requirements of a business.

There may sometimes be uncertainty regarding whether a transaction is not a derivative. If not, the transaction might be a normal purchase or a normal sale. The characteristics of these transactions are:

- There is a probable physical settlement, such as the delivery of goods or services.
- There is documentation of the transaction, such as the basis for a decision that the contract will result in physical delivery.
- There is a clearly and closely related underlying.
- There are normal terms; that is, the terms of the contract are consistent with the terms of an organization's normal purchases and sales.

EXAMPLE

Winslow Refining enters into a contract to purchase crude oil at a pre-determined price on a future date. The intent is to process all of the acquired crude oil through the company's Houston refinery. Since this transaction is part of the normal usage requirements of the business, it is not a derivative instrument.

EXAMPLE

Just down the street from Winslow Refining is the headquarters of Burton Brothers Investments. Burton earns money by speculating on the price of crude oil. Burton enters into a futures contract to purchase 100,000 barrels of crude oil on August 10, and plans to net settle the contract on that date. Thus, Burton does not take delivery of the oil. By the end of June, the price of crude oil has increased by $2 per barrel, so Burton has (so far) earned a profit of $200,000 on the contract. Since this transaction is entirely speculative, the transaction is a derivative.

What is a Hedge?

Hedging is a risk reduction technique, under which an entity uses a derivative or similar instrument to offset future changes in the fair value or cash flows of an asset or liability. The ideal outcome of a hedge is when the distribution of probable outcomes is reduced, so that the size of any potential loss is reduced. The following exhibit shows the effect of hedging on the range of possible outcomes.

Impact of Hedging on Risk Outcome

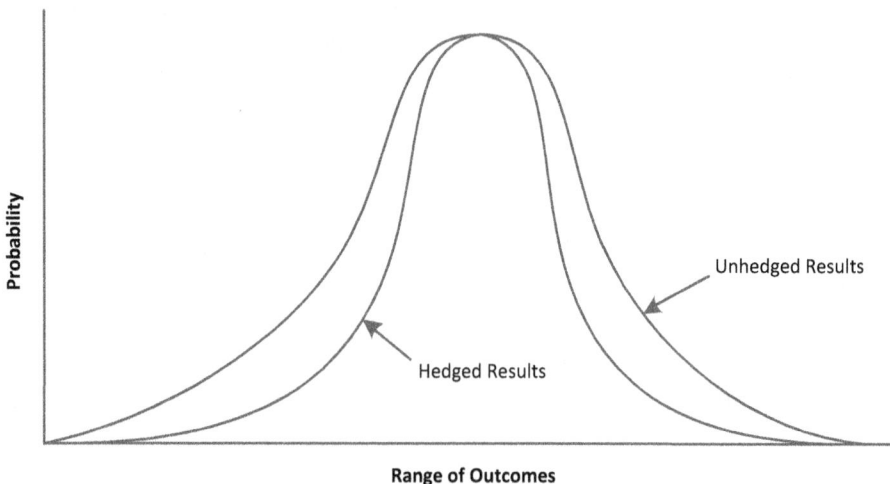

A hedged item can be any of the following individually or in a group with similar risk characteristics:

- A highly probable forecast transaction
- A net investment in a foreign operation
- A recognized asset
- A recognized liability
- An unrecognized firm commitment

It is quite acceptable to hedge a group of similar assets or liabilities, as long as the individual items in such a group share the same risk exposure that is being hedged.

Hedge effectiveness is the amount of the changes in the fair value or cash flows of a hedged item that are offset by changes in the fair value or cash flows of a hedging instrument. A highly effective hedging transaction is one in which the net effect of a pairing of a hedged item and a hedging instrument is close to zero.

What is Risk?

Risk is the probability of an outcome in which a loss occurs. In a business environment, one might engage in many transactions where there is a probability of a loss occurring, but usually this is a small probability in comparison to the probability of a profit. For example, a company may invest its excess cash in equity securities, partially to earn dividend income, and partially to take the chance that the securities will increase in value during the holding period. There is a slight risk that the issuer will buck its historical practices and refuse to pay a dividend, but there is a much greater risk that the securities will decline in value during the holding period – the decline in value is a risk that the company treasurer should consider before buying the securities. The type of risk noted in the example is called *financial risk*, which is the risk that changes in the markets will have a negative impact on the profits of a business.

Besides the risk of an equity investment declining in value, there are other instances where financial risk can arise. The following sub-sections illustrate several examples of financial risk.

Foreign Exchange Risk

When a business buys or sells across borders, it may need to use a foreign currency to settle these transactions. If so, the exchange rate between the entity's home currency and the foreign currency is continually changing. This means there is a risk that the company could be paid less by a customer than it is expecting, or be required to pay more to a supplier than it is expecting. An adverse change in an exchange rate could potentially wipe out the profit on a business deal.

There are several types of foreign exchange risk. A company may incur *transaction exposure*, which is derived from changes in foreign exchange rates between the dates when a transaction is booked and when it is settled. For example, a company in the United States may sell goods to a company in the United Kingdom, to be paid in pounds having a value at the booking date of $100,000. Later, when the customer pays the company, the exchange rate has changed, resulting in a payment in pounds that translates to a $95,000 sale. Thus, the foreign exchange rate change related to a transaction has created a $5,000 loss for the seller. The following table shows the impact of transaction exposure on different scenarios.

Risk When Transactions Denominated in Foreign Currency

	Import Goods	Export Goods
Home currency weakens	Loss	Gain
Home currency strengthens	Gain	Loss

When a company has foreign subsidiaries, it denominates the recorded amount of their assets and liabilities in the currency of the country in which the subsidiaries generate and expend cash. This *functional currency* is typically the local currency of the country in which a subsidiary operates. When the company reports its consolidated results, it converts these valuations to the home currency of the parent company, which may suffer a loss if exchange rates have declined from the last time when the financial statements were consolidated. This type of risk is known as *translation exposure*.

EXAMPLE

Suture Corporation has a subsidiary located in England, which has its net assets denominated in pounds. The home currency of Suture is U.S. dollars. At year-end, when the parent company consolidates the financial statements of its subsidiaries, the U.S. dollar has depreciated in comparison to the pound, resulting in a decline in the value of the subsidiary's net assets.

The following table shows the impact of translation exposure on different scenarios.

Risk When Net Assets Denominated in Foreign Currency

	Assets	Liabilities
Home currency weakens	Gain	Loss
Home currency strengthens	Loss	Gain

Interest Rate Risk

When interest rates rise, this increases the cost of interest payments for a business that holds a variable rate loan. Or, if interest rates fall, this reduces the market value of any bond investments that a business may have. In the latter case, the value of a bond drops when the interest rate that it pays is now less than the market interest rate; in order to increase their effective yield, investors must bid less to purchase a lower-paying bond.

More specifically, here are several different forms of interest rate risk:

- *Absolute rate changes*. The market rate of interest will move up or down over time, resulting in immediate variances from the interest rates paid or earned by a company.
- *Reinvestment risk*. Investments must be periodically re-invested and debt re-issued. If interest rates happen to be unfavorable during one of these rollover periods, a company will be forced to accept whatever interest rate is available.
- *Yield curve risk*. The yield curve shows the relationship between short-term and long-term interest rates, and typically slopes upward to indicate that long-term debt carries a higher interest rate to reflect the risk to the lender associated with such debt. If the yield curve steepens, flattens, or declines, these relationships change the debt duration that a company should use in its borrowing and investing strategies.

Interest risk is a particular concern for those businesses using large amounts of debt to fund their operations, since even a small increase in the interest rate could have a profound impact on profits, when multiplied by the volume of debt employed. Further, a sudden boost in interest expense could worsen a company's interest coverage ratio, which is a common covenant in loan agreements, and which could trigger a loan termination if the minimum ratio covenant is not met.

Credit Risk

Credit risk is the risk that a borrower will not pay back a loan, or that the counterparty to a contract will not pay. For most businesses, this risk really refers to the chance that a customer will not pay an invoice. A less-likely version of this risk is that the issuer of a security is unable to make scheduled payments to the debt holders. To deal with the latter case, a security is assigned a credit rating by a credit rating agency, such as Standard & Poor's, Moody's Investors Service, or Fitch Ratings. The ratings issued by these agencies are used by investors to determine the price at which to buy debt (usually bonds). The rating classifications used by the agencies vary from each other to some extent. The following table presents a comparison of the credit rating classifications of the three largest agencies. Debt issuances rated as investment grade in the table are considered suitable for investment purposes. The ratings classified as speculative are generally avoided by those entities looking for safe investments.

Credit Rating Comparison

Risk Level	Moody's	Standard & Poor's	Fitch
Investment grade:			
(highest investment grade)	Aaa	AAA	AAA
	Aa1	AA+	AA+
	Aa2	AA	AA
	Aa3	AA-	AA-
	A1	A+	A+
	A2	A	A
	A3	A-	A-
	Baa1	BBB+	BBB+
	Baa2	BBB	BBB
(lowest investment grade)	Baa3	BBB-	BBB-
Speculative grade:			
(highest speculative grade)	Ba1	BB+	BB+
	Ba2	BB	BB
	Ba3	BB-	BB-
	B1	B+	B+
	B2	B	B
	B3	B-	B-
	Caa1	CCC+	CCC+

Note: There are additional lower speculative grades than those listed in this table.

Another variation on credit risk is that a business enters into a derivative contract with a third party, and the third party does not pay the net settlement amount owed to the company.

Foreign Exchange Risk Management Alternatives

As noted in the last section, a company is at risk of incurring a loss due to fluctuations in any exchange rates that it must buy or sell as part of its business transactions. What can be done? Valid steps can range from no action at all to the active use of several types of hedges. In the following sub-sections, we address the multitude of options available to mitigate foreign exchange-related risks. As you peruse these options, keep in mind that the most sophisticated response is not necessarily the best response. In many cases, the circumstances may make it quite acceptable to take on some degree of risk, rather than engaging in a hedging strategy that is not only expensive, but also difficult to understand.

Take No Action

There are many situations where a company rarely engages in transactions that involve foreign exchange, and so does not want to spend time investigating how to reduce risk. There are other situations where the amounts of foreign exchange involved are so small that the risk level is immaterial. In either case, a company will be tempted to take no action, which may be a reasonable course of action. The question to consider is, at what level of foreign exchange activity should a business begin to consider risk management alternatives?

The question cannot be answered without having an understanding of a company's *risk capacity*. Risk capacity is the maximum amount of a loss that a business can sustain before a financial crisis is triggered. The following are examples of maximum losses:

- A loss that would require the tapping of all remaining borrowing capacity
- A loss that would breach one or more debt covenants
- A loss that would reduce capital levels below those mandated by regulatory authorities

The preceding examples provide hard quantitative numbers for a firm's total risk capacity, all of which threaten the company's existence. This does not mean that management should routinely expose a business to threat levels that could destroy it. Instead, it is necessary to arrive at a much less quantitative number, which is the maximum risk tolerance that management is willing to operate under on an ongoing basis before it will take steps to reduce risk. The risk tolerance figure is likely to be far lower than total risk capacity – perhaps just 5% or 10% of a firm's risk capacity. The exact amount of risk tolerance will depend upon the willingness of managers to accept risk. A more entrepreneurially inclined group may be willing to bet the company on risky situations, while professional managers will probably begin managing risk at lower tolerance levels.

Avoid Risk

A company can avoid some types of risk by altering its strategy to completely sidestep the risk. Complete avoidance of a specific product, geographic region, or business line is an entirely reasonable alternative under the following circumstances:

- The potential loss from a risk condition is very high
- The probability of loss from a risk condition is very high
- It is difficult to develop a hedge against a risk
- The offsetting potential for profit does not offset the risk that will be incurred

For example, a company located in the United States buys the bulk of its supplies in China, and is required under its purchasing contracts to pay suppliers in yuan. If the company does not want to undertake the risk of exchange rate fluctuations in the yuan, it can consider altering its supply chain, so that it purchases within its home country, rather than in China. This alignment of sales and purchases within the same country to avoid foreign currency transactions is known as an *operational hedge*.

As another example, a company wants to sell products into a market where the government has just imposed severe restrictions on the cross-border transfer of funds out of the country. The government also has a history of nationalizing industries that had been privately-owned. Under these circumstances, it makes little sense for the company to sell into the new market if it cannot extract its profits, and if its assets in the country are subject to expropriation.

Shift Risk

When a company is either required to pay or receive payment in a foreign currency, it is taking on the risk associated with changes in the foreign currency exchange rate. This risk can be completely eliminated by requiring customers to pay in the company's home currency, or suppliers to accept payment in the company's home currency. This is a valid option when the company is a large one that can force this system of payment onto its suppliers, or when it sells a unique product that forces customers to accept the company's terms.

Another possibility is to charge business partners for any changes in the exchange rate between the date of order placement and the shipment date. This is an extremely difficult business practice to enforce, for the following reasons:

- *Continual rebillings*. There will always be some degree of variation in exchange rates between the order date and shipment date, so it is probable that a company would have to issue an invoice related to exchange rate adjustments for every order, or at least include a line item for the change in every invoice.
- *Two-way rebillings*. If a company is going to insist on billing for its exchange rate losses, it is only fair that it pay back its business partners when exchange rates shift in its favor.
- *Purchase order limitations*. Customers routinely place orders using a purchase order that only authorizes a certain spending level. If the company later issues an incremental billing that exceeds the total amount authorized for a purchase, the customer will probably not pay the company.

To mitigate these issues, billing a business partner for a change in exchange rates should only be enacted if the change is sufficiently large to breach a contractually-agreed minimum level. The minimum level should be set so that this additional billing is a rare event.

EXAMPLE

An outsourcing company enters into long-term services contracts with its customers, and so is at considerable foreign exchange risk. It offers customers a fixed price contract within a 5% currency trading band, outside of which customers share the risk with the company. If the company gains from a currency shift outside of the trading band, it discounts the contract price.

The conditions under which currency risk can be shifted elsewhere are not common ones. Most companies will find that if they insist on only dealing in their home currencies, such behavior will either annoy suppliers or drive away customers. Thus, we will continue with other risk management actions that will be more palatable to a company's business partners.

Time Compression

Large variations in exchange rates are more likely to occur over longer periods of time than over shorter periods of time. Thus, it may be possible to reduce the risk of exchange rate fluctuations by reducing the contractually-mandated payment period. For example, 30 day payment terms could be compressed to 10 or 15 days. However, delays in shipping, customs inspections, and resistance from business partners can make it difficult to achieve a compressed payment schedule. Also, a customer being asked to accept a shorter payment schedule may attempt to push back with lower prices or other benefits, which increases the cost of this option.

The time compression concept can take the form of a company policy that does not allow standard credit terms to foreign customers that exceed a certain number of days. By doing so, a company can at least minimize the number of days during which exchange rates can fluctuate.

Build Reserves

If company management believes that there is just as great a risk of a gain as a loss on a currency fluctuation, it may be willing to accept the downside risk in hopes of attaining an upside profit. If so, it is possible to build cash and debt reserves greater than what would normally be needed, against the possibility of an outsized loss. This may entail investing a large amount of cash in very liquid investments, or retaining extra cash that might otherwise be paid out in dividends or used for capital expenditures. Other options are to obtain an unusually large line of credit that can be called upon in the event of a loss, or selling more stock than would typically be needed for operational purposes.

Building reserves will protect a business from foreign exchange risk, but the cost of acquiring and maintaining those reserves is substantial. Cash that is kept on hand could have earned an investment, while a commitment fee must be paid for a line of credit, even if the line is never used. Similarly, investors who buy a company's stock expect to earn a return. Thus, there is a noticeable cost associated with building reserves.

Maintain Local Reserves

If the company is routinely engaging in the purchase and sale of goods and services within another country, the answer may be to maintain a cash reserve within that country, which is denominated in the local currency. Doing so eliminates the cost of repeatedly buying and selling currencies and paying the related conversion commissions. The downside of maintaining local reserves is that a company is still subject to translation risk, where it must periodically translate its local cash reserves into its home currency for financial reporting purposes – which carries with it the risk of recording a translation loss.

Hedging

When all operational and strategic alternatives have been exhausted, it is time to consider buying hedging instruments that offset the risk posed by specific foreign exchange positions. Hedging is accomplished by purchasing an offsetting currency exposure. For example, if a company has a liability to deliver 1 million euros in six months, it can hedge this risk by entering into a contract to purchase 1 million euros on the same date, so that it can buy and sell in the same currency on the same date.

One should decide what proportion of risk exposure to hedge, such as 100% of the booked exposure or 50% of the forecasted exposure. This gradually declining benchmark hedge ratio for forecasted periods is justifiable on the assumption that the level of forecast accuracy declines over time, so at least hedge against the minimum amount of exposure that is likely to occur. A high-confidence currency forecast with little expected volatility should be matched with a higher benchmark hedge ratio, while a questionable forecast might justify a much lower ratio.

Interest Rate Risk Management Alternatives

The primary objective of interest risk management is to keep fluctuations in interest rates from impacting company earnings. Management can respond to this objective in many ways, ranging from a conscious decision to take no action, passing through a number of relatively passive alternatives, and culminating in several active techniques for risk mitigation. We provide an overview of each option in this section.

Take No Action

There may be situations where a company has minimal investments that earn interest, or issues only minor amounts of debt. If so, it is certainly acceptable to not implement an aggressive risk management campaign related to interest rates. However, this state of affairs does not typically last for long, after which there will be some degree of risk related to interest rates. In anticipation of such an event, it is useful to model the amount of interest rate change that must occur before there will be a serious impact on company finances. Once that trigger point is known, one can begin to prepare any of the risk mitigation alternatives noted later in this section.

Avoid Risk

The risk associated with interest rates arises between external entities and a business; it does not arise between the subsidiaries of the same business. Thus, a company can act as its own bank to some extent, by providing intercompany lending arrangements at interest rates that are not subject to fluctuations. This is particularly useful in a multi-national corporation, where cash reserves in different currencies may be scattered throughout the business, and can be lent back and forth to cover immediate cash needs.

Another way to avoid risk is to operate the business in such a conservative manner that the company has no debt, thereby eliminating the risk associated with interest rates on debt. The same result can be achieved by using invested funds to pay off any outstanding debt. The main downside of the low-debt method is that a company may be constraining its growth by not taking advantage of a low-cost source of funds (i.e., debt).

Asset and Liability Matching

A key trigger for interest rate risk is when short-term debt is used to fund an asset that is expected to be held for a long period of time. In this situation, the short-term debt must be rolled over multiple times during the life span of the asset or until the debt is paid off, introducing the risk that each successive debt rollover will result in an increased interest rate. To avoid this risk, arrange for financing that approximately matches the useful life of the underlying asset. Thus, spending $1 million for a machine that is expected to have a useful life of 10 years should be funded with a loan that also has a 10-year life.

Hedging

Interest rate hedging is the practice of acquiring financial instruments whose effects offset those of the underlying scenario causing interest rate fluctuations, so that the net effect is minimized rate fluctuations. Hedges fall into two categories:

- *Forward rate agreements and futures.* These financial instruments are designed to lock in an interest rate, so that changes in the actual interest rate above or below the baseline interest rate do not impact a business. These instruments do not provide any flexibility for taking advantage of favorable changes in interest rates.
- *Options.* These financial instruments only lock in an interest rate if the holder wants to do so, thereby presenting the possibility of benefiting from a favorable change in an interest rate.

Credit Risk Management Alternatives

The management of credit through non-hedging activities has been established for quite some time, and encompasses the activities noted in the following sub-sections.

Take No Action

The most common action that a business takes to deal with its credit risk is none at all. Instead, management accepts a certain amount of bad debt from nonpaying customers. There is likely to be a long history of bad debt losses that a business builds up over time, which management assumes will continue into the future. Thus, a certain proportion of sales is assumed to be bad debts, and that assumption is built into the financial models of the business.

Alter the Credit Policy

The first step in minimizing credit risk is increasing the effort expended to examine credit requests by customers. If high-risk customers can be spotted in advance, then the amount of credit granted will be reduced or eliminated, resulting in greatly reduced bad debts. This means that a prime risk management area is the credit department. To reduce risk, a business can tighten its credit policy, which leads to either a reduction in the total amount of credit granted, a compression of payment terms to encompass fewer days, or a combination of the two. Taking this conservative approach can have the negative effect of reducing total sales and total profits, since some higher-risk customers could be driven away who might have been able to pay. Consequently, alterations to the existing credit policy are usually made with great caution.

Enhance Collection Activities

A business can allocate more funds to the collections department. By doing so, more staff time and technology can be focused on late payers. By increasing the pressure on customers, the assumption is that cash will be collected sooner, and therefore the proportion of bad debts to sales will decline. This logic works to a certain extent, but at some point the cost of adding more funds to the collections department will not yield a corresponding decline in bad debts. Thus, there is a cost-benefit relationship that dictates the extent to which collection activities can be improved.

Foreign Exchange Hedging Instruments

This section describes a number of methods for hedging foreign currency transactions. The first type of hedge, which is a loan denominated in a foreign currency, is designed to offset translation risk. The remaining hedges target the transaction risk related to the currency fluctuations associated with either specific or aggregated business transactions.

Loan Denominated in a Foreign Currency

When a company is at risk of recording a loss from the translation of assets and liabilities into its home currency, it can hedge the risk by obtaining a loan denominated in the functional currency in which the assets and liabilities are recorded. The effect of this hedge is to neutralize any loss on translation of the subsidiary's net assets with a gain on translation of the loan, or vice versa.

EXAMPLE

Suture Corporation has a subsidiary located in London, and which does business entirely within England. Accordingly, the subsidiary's net assets are denominated in pounds. The net assets of the subsidiary are currently recorded at £10 million. To hedge the translation risk associated with these assets, Suture acquires a £10 million loan from a bank in London.

One month later, a change in the dollar/pound exchange rate results in a translation loss of $15,000 on the translation of the subsidiary's net assets into U.S. dollars. This amount is exactly offset by the translation gain of $15,000 on the liability associated with the £10 million loan.

> **Tip:** An ideal way to create an offsetting loan is to fund the purchase or expansion of a foreign subsidiary largely through the proceeds of a long-term loan obtained within the same country, so that the subsidiary's assets are approximately cancelled out by the amount of the loan.

There are two problems with this type of hedge. First, it can be difficult to obtain a loan in the country in which the net assets are located. Second, the company will incur an interest expense on a loan that it would not otherwise need, though the borrowed funds could be invested to offset the interest expense.

The Forward Contract

A forward contract is an agreement under which a business agrees to buy a certain amount of foreign currency on a specific future date, and at a predetermined exchange rate. Forward exchange rates can be obtained for twelve months into the future; quotes for major currency pairs can be obtained for as much as five to ten years in the future. The exchange rate is comprised of the following elements:

- The spot price of the currency
- The bank's transaction fee
- An adjustment (up or down) for the interest rate differential between the two currencies. In essence, the currency of the country having a lower interest rate will trade at a premium, while the currency of the country having a higher interest rate will trade at a discount. For example, if the domestic interest rate is lower than the rate in the other country, the bank acting as the counterparty adds points to the spot rate, which increases the cost of the foreign currency in the forward contract.

The calculation of the number of discount or premium points to subtract from or add to a forward contract is based on the following formula:

$$\text{Exchange rate} \times \text{Interest rate differential} \times \frac{\text{Days in contract}}{360} = \text{Premium or discount}$$

Thus, if the spot price of pounds per dollar were 1.5459 and there were a premium of 15 points for a forward contract with a 360-day maturity, the forward rate (not including a transaction fee) would be 1.5474.

By entering into a forward contract, a company can ensure that a definite future liability can be settled at a specific exchange rate. Forward contracts are typically customized, and arranged between a company and its bank. The bank will require a partial payment to initiate a forward contract, as well as final payment shortly before the settlement date.

EXAMPLE

Suture Corporation has acquired computer software from a company in the United Kingdom, which Suture must pay for in 90 days in the amount of £220,000. To hedge against the risk of an unfavorable change in exchange rates during the intervening 90 days, Suture enters into a forward contract with its bank to buy £220,000 in 90 days, at the current exchange rate.

90 days later, the exchange rate has indeed taken a turn for the worse, but Suture's treasurer is indifferent, since he obtains the £220,000 needed for the purchase transaction based on the exchange rate in existence when the contract with the supplier was originally signed.

A forward contract is designed to have a specific settlement date, but the business transaction to which it relates may not be so timely. For example, a business has a contract to sell £10,000 in 60 days, but may not be able to do so if it has not yet received funds from a customer. A *forward window contract* is designed to work around this variability in the timing of receipts from customers by incorporating a range of settlement dates. One can then wait for a cash receipt and trigger settlement of the forward contract immediately thereafter.

The primary difficulties with forward contracts relate to their being customized transactions that are designed specifically for two parties. Because of this level of customization, it is difficult for either party to offload the contract to a third party. Also, the level of customization makes it difficult to compare offerings from different banks, so there is a tendency for banks to build unusually large fees into these contracts. Finally, a company may find that the underlying transaction for which a forward contract was created has been cancelled, leaving the contract still to be settled. If so, one can enter into a second forward contract, whose net effect is to offset the first forward contract. Though the bank will charge fees for both contracts, this arrangement will settle the company's obligations.

The Futures Contract

A futures contract is similar in concept to a forward contract, in that a business can enter into a contract to buy or sell currency at a specific price on a future date. The difference is that futures contracts are traded on an exchange, so these contracts are for standard amounts and durations. An initial deposit into a margin account is required to initiate a futures contract. The contract is then repriced each day, and if cumulative losses drain the margin account, a company is required to add more funds to the margin account. If the company does not respond to a margin call, the exchange closes out the contract.

Given that futures contracts are standardized, they may not exactly match the timing and amounts of an underlying transaction that is being hedged, which can lead to over- or under-hedging. However, since these contracts are traded on an exchange, it is easier to trade them than forward contracts, which allows one to easily unwind a hedge position earlier than its normal settlement date.

The Currency Option

An option gives its owner the right, but not the obligation, to buy or sell an asset at a certain price (known as the *strike price*), either on or before a specific date. In exchange for this right, the buyer pays an up-front premium to the seller. The income earned by the seller is restricted to the premium payment received, while the buyer has a theoretically unlimited profit potential, depending upon the future direction of the relevant exchange rate.

Currency options are available for the purchase or sale of currencies within a certain future date range, with the following variations available for the option contract:

- *American option.* The option can be exercised on any date within the option period, so that delivery is two business days after the exercise date.
- *European option.* The option can only be exercised on the expiry date, which means that delivery will be two business days after the expiry date.
- *Burmudan option.* The option can only be exercised on certain predetermined dates.

The holder of an option will exercise it when the strike price is more favorable than the current market rate, which is called being *in-the-money*. If the strike price is less favorable than the current market rate, this is called being *out-of-the-money*, in which case the option holder will not exercise the option. If the option holder is inattentive, it is possible that an in-the-money option will not be exercised prior to its expiry date. Notice of option exercise must be given to the counterparty by the notification date stated in the option contract.

A currency option provides two key benefits:

- *Loss prevention.* An option can be exercised to hedge the risk of loss, while still leaving open the possibility of benefiting from a favorable change in exchange rates.
- *Date variability.* One can exercise an option within a predetermined date range, which is useful when there is uncertainty about the exact timing of the underlying exposure.

There are a number of factors that enter into the price of a currency option, which can make it difficult to ascertain whether a quoted option price is reasonable. These factors are:

- The difference between the designated strike price and the current spot price. The buyer of an option can choose a strike price that suits his specific circumstances. A strike price that is well away from the current spot price will cost less, since the likelihood of exercising the option is low. However, setting such a strike price means that the buyer is willing to absorb the loss associated with a significant change in the exchange rate before seeking cover behind an option.
- The current interest rates for the two currencies during the option period.

- The duration of the option.
- The volatility of the market. This is the expected amount by which the currency is expected to fluctuate during the option period, with higher volatility making it more likely that an option will be exercised. Volatility is a guesstimate, since there is no quantifiable way to predict it.
- The willingness of counterparties to issue options.

Banks generally allow an option exercise period of no more than three months. Multiple partial currency deliveries within a currency option can be arranged.

Exchange traded options for standard quantities are available. This type of option eliminates the risk of counterparty failure, since the clearing house operating the exchange guarantees the performance of all options traded on the exchange.

EXAMPLE

Suture Corporation has an obligation to buy £250,000 in three months. Currently, the forward rate for the British pound is 1.5000 U.S. dollars, so that it should require $375,000 to buy the £250,000 in 90 days. If the pound depreciates, Suture will be able to buy pounds for less than the $375,000 that it currently anticipates spending, but if the pound appreciates, Suture will have to spend more to acquire the £250,000.

Suture's treasurer elects to buy an option, so that he can hedge against the appreciation of the pound, while leaving open the prospect of profits to be gained from any depreciation in the pound. The cost of an option with a strike price of 1.6000 U.S. dollars per pound is $3,000.

Three months later, the pound has appreciated against the dollar, with the price having changed to 1.75 U.S. dollars per pound. The treasurer exercises the option, and spends $400,000 for the requisite number of pounds (calculated as £250,000 × 1.6000). If he had not purchased the option, the purchase would instead have cost $437,500 (calculated as £250,000 × 1.7500). Thus, Suture saved $34,500 by using a currency option (calculated as the savings of $37,500, less the $3,000 cost of the option).

Currency options are particularly valuable during periods of high currency price volatility. Unfortunately from the perspective of the buyer, high volatility equates to higher option prices, since there is a higher probability that the counterparty will have to make a payment to the option buyer.

The Cylinder Option

Two options can be combined to create a *cylinder option*. One option is priced above the current spot price of the target currency, while the other option is priced below the spot price. The gain from exercising one option is used to partially offset the cost of the other option, thereby reducing the overall cost of the hedge. In effect, the upside potential offered by one option is being sold for a premium payment in order to finance the protection afforded by the opposing option.

The cylinder option is configured so that a company can acquire the right to buy currency at a specified price (a call option) and sell an option to a counterparty to buy currency from the company at a specified price (a put option), usually as of the expiry date. The premium the company pays for the purchased call is partially offset by the premium payable to the company for the put option that it sold.

If the market exchange rate remains between the boundaries established by the two currency options, the company never uses its options and instead buys or sells currency on the open market to fulfill its currency needs. If the market price breaches the strike price of the call option, the company exercises the call option and buys currency at the designated strike price. Conversely, if the market price breaches the strike price of the put option, the counterparty exercises its option to sell the currency to the company.

A variation on the cylinder option is to construct call and put options that are very close together, so that the premium cost of the call is very close to the premium income generated by the put, resulting in a near-zero net hedging cost to the company. The two options have to be very close together for the zero cost option to work, which means that the effective currency price range being hedged is quite small.

Swaps

If a company has or expects to have an obligation to make a payment in a foreign currency, it can arrange to swap currency holdings with a third party that already has the required currency. The two entities engage in a swap transaction by agreeing upon an initial swap date, the date when the cash positions will be reversed back to their original positions, and an interest rate that reflects the comparative differences in interest rates between the two countries in which the entities are located.

Another use for a currency swap is when a forward exchange contract has been delayed. In this situation, one would normally sell to a counterparty the currency that it has just obtained through the receipt of an account receivable. If, however, the receivable has not yet been paid, the company can enter into a swap agreement to obtain the required currency and meet its immediate obligation under the forward exchange contract. Later, when the receivable is eventually paid, the company can reverse the swap, returning funds to the counterparty.

A swap arrangement may be for just a one-day period, or extend out for several years into the future. Swap transactions generally do not occur in amounts of less than $5 million, so this technique is not available to smaller businesses.

A potentially serious problem with swaps is the prospect of a default by the counterparty. If there is a default, the company once again assumes its foreign currency liability, and must now scramble to find an alternative hedge.

Interest Rate Hedging Instruments

This section describes a number of methods for hedging transactions in which there is a risk of an adverse change in interest rates.

The Forward Rate Agreement

A forward rate agreement (FRA) is an agreement between two parties to lock in a specific interest rate for a designated period of time, which usually spans just a few months. Under an FRA, the parties are protecting against opposing exposures: the FRA buyer wants to protect against an increase in the interest rate, while the FRA seller wants to protect against a decrease in the interest rate. Any payout under an FRA is based on a change in the reference interest rate from the interest rate stated in the contract (the FRA rate). An FRA is not related to a specific loan or investment – it simply provides interest rate protection.

The FRA rate is based on the yield curve, where interest rates usually increase for instruments having longer maturities. This means that the FRA rate typically increases for periods further in the future.

Several date-specific terms are referred to in a forward rate agreement, and are crucial to understanding how the FRA concept works. These terms are:

1. *Contract date*. The date on which the FRA begins.
2. *Expiry date*. The date on which any variance between the market rate and the reference rate is calculated.
3. *Settlement date*. The date on which the interest variance is paid by one counterparty to the other.
4. *Maturity date*. The final date of the date range that underlies the FRA contract.

In essence, these four dates anchor the two time periods covered by an FRA. The first period, which begins with the contract date and ends with the expiry date, spans the term of the contract. The second period begins with the settlement date and ends with the maturity date, and spans the period that underlies the contract. This date range is shown graphically in the following example.

Relevant FRA Dates

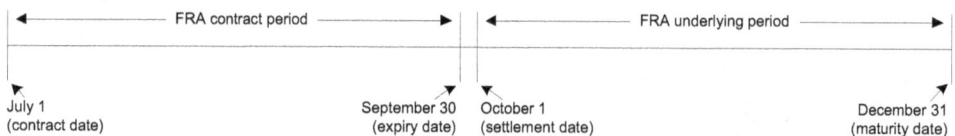

| ◄─────── FRA contract period ───────► | ◄─────── FRA underlying period ───────► |
| July 1 (contract date) | September 30 (expiry date) | October 1 (settlement date) | December 31 (maturity date) |

The FRA rate is based on a future period, such as the period starting in one month and ending in four months, which is said to have a "1 × 4" FRA term, and has an effective term of three months. Similarly, a contract starting in three months and ending in six months is said to have a "3 × 6" FRA term, and also has an effective term of three months.

At the *beginning* of the designated FRA period, the interest rate stated in the contract is compared to the reference rate. The reference rate is usually a well-known interest rate index. If the reference rate is higher, the seller makes a payment to the FRA buyer, based on the incremental difference in interest rates and the notional amount of the contract. The payment calculation is shown in the following example. If the reference rate is lower than the interest rate stated in the contract, the buyer makes a payment to the FRA seller. The payment made between the counterparties must be discounted to its present value, since the payment is associated with the FRA underlying period that has not yet happened. Thus, the discount assumes that the money would actually be due on the maturity date, but is payable on the settlement date (which may be months before the maturity date). The calculation for discounting the payment between counterparties is:

$$\frac{\text{Settlement amount}}{1 + (\text{Days in FRA underlying period}/360 \text{ Days} \times \text{Reference rate})} = \text{Discounted Payment}$$

The reason why the contract payment is calculated at the *beginning* of the designated FRA period is that the risk being hedged by the contract was from the initial contract date until the date on which the FRA buyer expects to borrow money and lock in an interest rate. For example, a company may enter into an FRA in January, because it is uncertain of what the market interest rate will be in April, when it intends to borrow funds; the period at risk is therefore from January through April. The following example illustrates the concept.

EXAMPLE

Suture Corporation has a legal commitment to borrow $50 million in two months, and for a period of three months. Suture's treasurer is concerned that there may be an increase in the interest rate during the two-month period prior to borrowing the $50 million. The treasurer elects to hedge the risk of an increase in the interest rate by purchasing a three-month FRA, starting in two months. A broker quotes a rate of 5.50%. Suture enters into an FRA at the 5.50% interest rate, with 3rd National Bank as the counterparty. The notional amount of the contract is for $50 million.

Two months later, the reference rate is 6.00%, so 3rd National pays Suture the difference between the contract rate and reference rate, which is 0.50%. At the same time, Suture borrows $50 million at the market rate (which happens to match the reference rate) of 6.00%. Because of the FRA, Suture's effective borrowing rate is 5.50%.

The amount paid by 3rd National to Suture is calculated as:

(Reference rate – FRA rate) × (FRA days/360 days) × Notional amount = Profit or loss

or

(6.00% - 5.50%) × (90 days/360 days) × $50 million = $62,500

Since the payment is made at the beginning of the borrowing period, rather than at its end, the $62,500 payment is discounted and its present value paid. The discounting calculation for the settlement amount is:

$$\frac{\$62,500}{1 + (90/360 \text{ Days} \times 6.00\%)} = \$61,576.35$$

What if the reference rate had fallen by 0.50%, instead of increasing? Then Suture would have paid 3rd National the discounted amount of $62,500, rather than the reverse. Suture would also end up borrowing the $50 million at the new market rate of 5.00%. When the payment to 3rd National is combined with the reduced 5.00% interest rate, Suture will still be paying a 5.50% interest rate, which is what it wanted all along.

From the buyer's perspective, the result of an FRA is that it pays the expected interest rate – no higher, and no lower.

The Futures Contract

An interest rate futures contract is conceptually similar to a forward contract, except that it is traded on an exchange, which means that it is for a standard amount and duration. The standard size of a futures contract is $1 million, so multiple contracts may need to be purchased to create a hedge for a specific loan or investment amount. The pricing for futures contracts starts at a baseline figure of 100, and declines based on the implied interest rate in a contract. For example, if a futures contract has an implied interest rate of 5.00%, the price of that contract will be 95.00. The calculation of the profit or loss on a futures contract is derived as follows:

Notional contract amount × Contract duration/360 Days × (Ending price – Beginning price)

Hedging is not perfect, since the notional amount of a contract may vary from the actual amount of funding that a company wants to hedge, resulting in a modest amount of either over- or under-hedging. For example, hedging a $15.4 million position will require the purchase of either 15 or 16 $1 million contracts. There may also be differences between the time period required for a hedge and the actual hedge period as stated in a futures contract. For example, if there is a seven month exposure to be hedged, one could acquire two consecutive three-month contracts, and elect to have the seventh month be unhedged.

Tip: If the buyer wants to protect against interest rate variability for a longer period, such as for the next year, it is possible to buy a series of futures contracts covering consecutive periods, so that coverage is achieved for the entire time period.

EXAMPLE

The treasurer of Suture Corporation wants to hedge an investment of $10 million. To do so, he sells 10 three-month futures contracts with contract terms of three months. The current three-month reference rate is 3.50% and the 3 × 6 forward rate is 3.75%. These contracts are currently listed on the Chicago Mercantile Exchange at 96.25, which is calculated as 100 minus the 3.75% forward rate.

When the futures contracts expire, the forward rate has declined to 3.65%, so that the contracts are now listed at 96.35 (calculated as 100 – the 3.65 percent forward rate). By engaging in this hedge, Suture has earned a profit of $2,500, which is calculated as follows:

$$\$10,000,000 \times (90/360) \times (0.9635 \text{ Ending price} - 0.9625 \text{ Beginning price})$$

$$= \$2,500$$

When the buyer purchases a futures contract, a minimum amount must initially be posted in a margin account to ensure performance under the contract terms. It may be necessary to fund the margin account with additional cash (a *margin call*) if the market value of the contract declines over time (margin accounts are revised daily, based on the market closing price). If the buyer cannot provide additional funding in the event of a contract decline, the futures exchange closes out the contract prior to its normal termination date. Conversely, if the market value of the contract increases, the net gain is credited to the buyer's margin account. On the last day of the contract, the exchange marks the contract to market and settles the accounts of the buyer and seller. Thus, transfers between buyers and sellers over the life of a contract are essentially a zero-sum game, where one party directly benefits at the expense of the other.

It is also possible to enter into a bond futures contract, which can be used to hedge interest rate risk. For example, a business that has borrowed funds can hedge against rising interest rates by selling a bond futures contract. Then, if interest rates do in fact rise, the resulting gain on the contract will offset the higher interest rate that the borrower is paying. Conversely, if interest rates subsequently fall, the borrower will experience a loss on the contract, which will offset the lower interest rate now being paid. Thus, the net effect of the contract is that the borrower locks in the beginning interest rate through the period of the contract.

Tip: A bond futures contract is not a perfect hedge, for it is also impacted by changes in the credit rating of the bond issuer.

When a purchased futures contract expires, it is customary to settle it by selling a futures contract that has the same delivery date. Conversely, if the original contract was sold to a counterparty, then the seller can settle the contract by buying a futures contract that has the same delivery date.

The following table notes the key differences between forward rate agreements and futures contracts. Similarities between the two instruments are excluded from the table.

Differences between a Futures Contract and FRA

Feature	Futures Contract	Forward Rate Agreement
Trading platform	Exchange-based	Between two parties
Counterparty	The exchange	Single counterparty
Collateral	Margin account	None
Agreement	Standardized	Modified
Settlement	Daily mark to market	On expiry date

The preceding table reveals two key differences between a futures contract and an FRA. First, there can be significant counterparty risk in an FRA, since the contract period can be lengthy, and financial conditions can change markedly over that time. Second, a futures contract is settled every day, which can create pressure to fund a margin call if there are significant losses on the contract.

Interest Rate Swaps

An interest rate swap is a customized contract between two parties to swap two schedules of cash flows that could extend for anywhere from one to 25 years, and which represent interest payments. Only the interest rate obligations are swapped, not the underlying loans or investments from which the obligations are derived. The counterparties are usually a company and a bank. There are many types of rate swaps; we will confine this discussion to a swap arrangement where one schedule of cash flows is based on a floating interest rate, and the other is based on a fixed interest rate. For example, a five-year schedule of cash flows based on a fixed interest rate may be swapped for a five-year schedule of cash flows based on a floating interest rate that is tied to a reference rate.

The most common reason to engage in an interest rate swap is to exchange a variable-rate payment for a fixed-rate payment, or vice versa. Thus, a company that has only been able to obtain a floating-rate loan can effectively convert the loan to a fixed-rate loan through an interest rate swap. This approach is especially attractive when a borrower is only able to obtain a fixed-rate loan by paying a premium, but can combine a variable-rate loan and an interest rate swap to achieve a fixed-rate loan at a lower price.

A company may want to take the reverse approach and swap its fixed interest payments for floating payments. This situation arises when management believes that interest rates will decline during the swap period, and wants to take advantage of the lower rates.

A swap contract is settled through a multi-step process, which is:

1. Calculate the payment obligation of each party, typically once every six months through the life of the swap arrangement.
2. Determine the variance between the two amounts.
3. The party whose position is improved by the swap arrangement pays the variance to the party whose position is degraded by the swap arrangement.

Thus, a company continues to pay interest to its banker under the original lending agreement, while the company either accepts a payment from the rate swap counterparty, or issues a payment to the counterparty, with the result being that the net amount of interest paid by the company is the amount planned by the business when it entered into the swap agreement.

EXAMPLE

Suture Corporation has a $15 million variable-rate loan outstanding that matures in two years. The current interest rate on the loan is 6.5%. Suture enters into an interest rate swap agreement with Big Regional Bank for a fixed-rate 7.0% loan with a $15 million notional amount. The first scheduled payment swap date is in six months. On that date, the variable rate on Suture's loan has increased to 7.25%. Thus, the total interest payments on the swap date are $543,750 for Suture and $525,000 for Big Regional. Since the two parties have agreed to swap payments, Big Regional pays Suture the difference between the two payments, which is $18,750.

Suture issues an interest payment of $543,750 to its bank. When netted with the cash inflow of $18,750 from Big Regional, this means that the net interest rate being paid by Suture is 7.0%.

Several larger banks have active trading groups that routinely deal with interest rate swaps. Most swaps involve sums in the millions of dollars, but some banks are willing to engage in swap arrangements involving amounts of less than $1 million. There is a counterparty risk with interest rate swaps, since one party could fail to make a contractually-mandated payment to the other party. This risk is of particular concern when a swap arrangement covers multiple years, since the financial condition of a counterparty could change dramatically during that time.

If there is general agreement in the marketplace that interest rates are headed in a certain direction, it will be more expensive to obtain a swap that protects against interest rate changes in the anticipated direction.

Interest Rate Options

An option gives its owner the right, but not the obligation, to trigger a contract. The contract can be either a call option or a put option. A *call option* related to interest rates protects the option owner from rising interest rates, while a *put option* protects the option owner from declining interest rates. The party selling an option does so in exchange for a one-time premium payment. The party buying an option is doing so to mitigate its risk related to a change in interest rates.

An interest rate option can be relatively inexpensive if there has been or is expected to be little volatility in interest rates, since the option seller does not expect interest rates to move enough for the option to be exercised. Conversely, if there has been or is expected to be considerable interest rate volatility, the option seller must assume that the option will be exercised, and so sets a higher price. Thus, periods of high interest rate volatility may make it cost-prohibitive to buy options.

Tip: An interest rate hedge using an option may not be entirely successful if the reference rate used for the option is not the same one used for the underlying loan. For example, the reference rate for an option may be SIBOR[1], while the rate used for the underlying loan may be a bank's prime rate. The result is a hedging mismatch that can create an unplanned gain or loss.

An interest rate option sets a *strike price*, which is a specific interest rate at which the option buyer can borrow or lend money. The contract also states the amount of funds that the option buyer can borrow or lend (the *notional amount*). Rate increases and declines are measured using a *reference rate*, which is typically a well-known interest rate index. There is also an option expiration date, or *expiry date*, after which the option is cancelled. The buyer can specify the exact terms needed to hedge an interest rate position with a customized option.

If an option buyer wants to be protected from increases in interest rates, a *cap* (or ceiling) is created. A cap is a consecutive series of options, all having the same strike price. The buyer of a cap is paid whenever the reference rate exceeds the cap strike price on an option expiry date. For example, if a company wants to hedge its interest risk for one year with a strike price of 6.50%, beginning on January 1, it can buy the following options:

Desired Coverage Period	Option Number	Expiry Date	Option Term	Strike Price
January - March	--	Not applicable*	Not available*	N/A*
April - June	1	April 1	4 to 6 months	6.50%
July – September	2	July 1	7 to 9 months	6.50%
October - December	3	October 1	10 to 12 months	6.50%

* There is no option available for the first three-month period, since the expiry date is at the beginning of the contract period; the expiry date would be reached immediately.

With a cap arrangement, the buyer is only subject to interest rate changes up to the cap, and is protected from rate changes above the cap if the reference rate exceeds the cap strike price on predetermined dates. If the reference interest rate is below the cap at the option expiration, the option buyer lets the option expire. However, if the

---

[1] Singapore Interbank Offered Rate

reference rate is above the cap, the buyer exercises the option, which means that the option seller must reimburse the buyer for the difference between the reference rate and the cap rate, multiplied by the notional amount of the contract.

A cap may be included in a loan agreement, such that the borrower is guaranteed not to pay more than a designated maximum interest rate over the term of the loan, or for a predetermined portion of the loan. In this case, the lender has paid for the cap, and will probably include its cost in the interest rate or fees associated with the loan.

To be protected from decreases in interest rates (for invested funds), a *floor* is structured into an option, so that the option buyer is paid if the reference rate declines below the floor strike rate.

EXAMPLE

Suture Corporation has a $25 million 3-month loan that currently carries a fixed interest rate of 7.00%. Suture's bank refuses to grant a fixed-rate loan for a longer time period, so Suture plans to continually roll over the loan every three months. Recently, short-term interest rates have been spiking, so the treasurer decides to purchase an interest rate cap that is set at 7.50%, and which is comprised of two consecutive options, each with a three-month term.

At the expiry date of the first option, the reference rate is 7.25%, which is below the cap strike rate. The treasurer lets the option expire unused and rolls over the short-term loan at the new 7.25% rate.

At the next option expiry date, the reference rate has risen to 7.75%, which is 0.25% above the cap strike rate. The treasurer exercises the option, which forces the counterparty to pay Suture for the difference between the cap strike rate and the reference rate. The calculation of the amount to be reimbursed is:

(Reference rate – Strike rate) × (Lending period/360 days) × Notional amount = Profit or loss

or

(7.75% - 7.50%) × (90/360) × $25 million = $15,625

Of course, the cost of the option reduces the benefits gained from an interest rate option, but still is useful for providing protection from outsized changes in interest rates.

Tip: From an analysis perspective, it is useful to include the premium on an option with the amount of interest paid on a loan and any proceeds or payments associated with an exercised option, in order to derive the aggregate interest rate on any associated debt being hedged.

The cylinder option described earlier for foreign exchange transactions can also be applied to interest rates. Under this concept, a company purchases a cap and sells a floor, with the current reference rate located between the two strike rates. The gain from exercising one option is used to partially offset the cost of the other option, which reduces the overall cost of the hedge. The three possible outcomes to this *collar* arrangement are:

1. The reference rate remains between the cap and floor, so neither option is exercised.
2. The reference rate rises above the cap, so the company is paid for the difference between the reference rate and the cap strike rate, multiplied by the notional amount of the contract.
3. The reference rate falls below the floor, so the company pays the option counterparty for the difference between the reference rate and the floor strike rate, multiplied by the notional amount of the contract.

The functioning of a collar arrangement is shown in the following exhibit, where the cap is set at 5% and the floor is set at 3%. No option is triggered until the reference rate drops to 2% in one of the later quarters, and again when it rises to 6%. In the first case, the company pays the 1% difference between the 3% floor and the 2% reference rate. In the latter case, the company is paid the 1% difference between the 5% cap and the 6% reference rate.

The Operation of an Interest Rate Collar

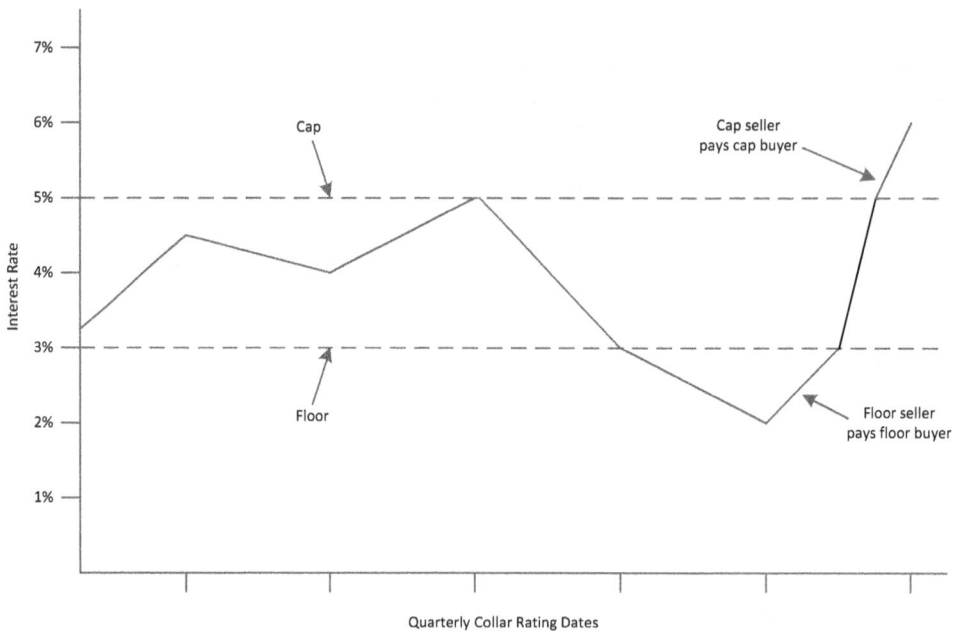

Quarterly Collar Rating Dates

From the perspective of a company using a collar arrangement, the net effect is that interest rates will fluctuate only within the bounds set by the cap and floor strike rates.

A variation on the interest rate option concept is to include a call feature in a debt issuance. A call feature allows a company to buy back its debt from debt holders. The feature is quite useful in cases where the market interest rate has fallen since debt was issued, so a company can refinance its debt at a lower interest rate. However, the presence of the call option makes investors wary about buying it, which tends to increase the effective interest rate at which they will buy the debt. Investor concerns can be mitigated to some extent by providing for a fairly long time period before the issuing company can trigger the call option, and especially if the call price is set somewhat higher than the current market price.

Interest Rate Swaptions

A swaption is an option on an interest rate swap arrangement. The buyer of a swaption has the right, but not the obligation, to enter into an interest rate swap. In essence, a swaption presents the option of being able to lock in a fixed interest rate or a variable interest rate (depending on the terms of the underlying swap arrangement). Thus, one may suspect that interest rates will begin to rise in the near future, and so enters into a swaption to take over a fixed interest rate. If interest rates do indeed rise, the swaption holder can exercise the swaption. If interest rates hold steady or decline, the swaption is allowed to expire without being exercised.

The two types of swaption are the *payer swaption* and the *receiver swaption*, which are defined as follows:

- *Payer swaption.* The buyer can enter into a swap where it pays the fixed interest rate side of the transaction.
- *Receiver swaption.* The buyer can enter into a swap where it pays the floating interest rate side of the transaction.

There is no formal exchange for swaptions, so each agreement is between two counterparties. This means that each party is exposed to the potential failure of the counterparty to make scheduled payments on the underlying swap. Consequently, it is prudent to only enter into these arrangements with counterparties with high credit ratings or other evidence of financial stability.

Swaption market participants are primarily large corporations, banks, and hedge funds. The most likely counterparty for a corporation is a large bank that has a group specializing in swaption arrangements.

Credit Risk Hedging Instruments

When a business is a risk of not being paid back, the usual approach is to mitigate this risk by altering internal credit review procedures. It is also possible to engage in credit default swaps, which shift the credit risk to a third party. Both concepts are described in the following sub-sections.

Credit Risk

A seller may find that it can shift some of the risk associated with its accounts receivable to a firm that provides credit insurance. Under a credit insurance policy, the insurer protects the seller against customer nonpayment. The insurer should be willing to provide coverage against customer nonpayment if a proposed customer clears its internal review process. Credit insurance offers the following benefits:

- *Increased credit.* A company may be able to increase the credit levels offered to its customers, thereby potentially increasing revenue.
- *Faster international deals.* An international sale might normally be delayed while the parties arrange a letter of credit, but can be completed faster with credit insurance.
- *Custom product coverage.* The insurance can cover the shipment of custom-made products, in case customers cancel their orders prior to delivery.
- *Reduced credit staff.* Credit insurance essentially shifts risk away from a business, so it is especially beneficial in companies that have an understaffed credit department that cannot adequately keep track of customer credit levels.
- *Knowledge.* A credit insurance firm specializes in the risk characteristics of various industries, and so may have deep knowledge about the risk profiles of individual customers, as well as aggregations of customers by region. This information is a useful supplement to other sources of information about customers.
- *Tax deductibility.* Credit insurance premiums are immediately deductible for tax purposes, whereas the allowance for doubtful accounts is only deductible when specific bad debts are recognized.

As is the case with all insurance policies, be sure to examine the terms of a credit insurance agreement for exclusions, to see what the insurer will not cover. In particular, coverage should include the receivables of customers that file for bankruptcy protection or simply go out of business.

Insurers will only provide coverage for legally sustainable debts, which are those receivables that are not disputed by the customer. If there is a dispute, the insurer will only provide coverage after the company has won a court judgment against the customer. The issue of a legally sustainable debt can be a serious one if a company has a track record of disputes with its customers over product quality, damaged goods, returns, and so forth.

Tip: It may be possible to offload the cost of credit insurance to customers by adding it to customer invoices. This is most likely to be acceptable for international deals, where a customer would otherwise be forced to obtain a letter of credit to pay for a transaction.

Insurers are more willing to provide coverage of accounts receivable if the seller is willing to take on a small part of the bad debt risk itself. This typically means that a customer default will result in the insurer reimbursing the seller, minus the amount of a 5% to 20% deductible. There may also be an annual aggregate deductible that requires the company to absorb a certain fixed amount of losses in a year before the insurer begins to pay reimbursements. Requiring a deductible means that the company continues to have an interest in only selling to credit-worthy customers.

EXAMPLE

Micron Metallic sells stamping machines to a variety of industrial customers. The company's credit insurance policy states that Micron will absorb the first $200,000 of bad debt losses in each calendar year, after which the insurer will pay 85% of all bad debts incurred, other than for invoices related to international sales, which are not covered by the policy. The policy also specifically excludes receivables related to ABC Company, which the insurer considers to be at an excessively high risk of default.

For some customers, or geographic regions subject to considerable political risk, a credit insurer may consider the risk to be so great that it will not provide coverage, or only at a high premium. If so, the credit manager must decide whether it is better for the company to assume the risk of these sales, or to pay the cost of the insurance to obtain coverage. Also, if the insurer discovers that the company's historical loss experience with its customers has been excessively high, it may require such a large premium that the company may conclude that insurance coverage is not a cost-effective form of risk reduction.

Insurers may only be willing to insure a certain amount of receivables per year with some customers. If the company chooses to sell additional amounts on credit to these designated customers, the company will sustain the entire incremental amount of credit risk. To avoid the additional risk, it is necessary to track the cumulative amount of credit sales to these customers on an ongoing basis.

Credit Default Swaps

A credit default swap (CDS) transfers credit exposure between parties. In essence, the seller of a CDS agrees to pay off a debt owed by a third party to the buyer of the CDS if the third party defaults on the debt. Thus, a CDS is a type of insurance, where the risk of default is shifted from the holder of the debt to the seller of the CDS. Common users of CDS instruments are pension funds, hedge funds, banks, and insurance companies. A knowledgeable CDS seller will not be willing to issue a CDS if the third party has a low credit rating, so the fee charged for a CDS should be quite expensive for higher-risk debt arrangements.

CDS arrangements are commonly used for all types of debt arrangements, including mortgage-backed securities, corporate debt, and municipal bonds.

A potential issue with CDS instruments is that the seller of a CDS could have liquidity problems and so may not be able to pay the buyer. This means that the risk of default switches back to the buyer of the CDS.

EXAMPLE

Micron Metallic wants to borrow $80 million from Currency Bank and will pay a spread of 100 basis points over the prime rate. The risk manager of Currency Bank is interested, but cannot justify making such a large loan to a single customer, since the bank incurs a significant credit risk. However, Currency Bank can buy a CDS for 30 basis points. Gulf Coast Insurance agrees to be the counterparty for a CDS, which means that Gulf Coast will pay Currency Bank if Micron defaults. In exchange, Gulf Coast will receive $240,000 per year (calculated as 30 basis points × $80,000,000) while the loan is outstanding.

Summary

In this chapter, we placed a significant amount of emphasis on non-derivative ways to mitigate risk, by (for example) shifting risk elsewhere, avoiding risk situations, and accepting small amounts of risk. This level of emphasis was used in order to remind the reader of the sensible alternatives that are available before electing to use derivative instruments. Derivatives can be difficult to understand, have arcane terminology, and can be expensive. Nonetheless, if it appears necessary to use derivatives, then explore the following chapter to learn about the equally complex accounting rules associated with derivatives and especially with hedging transactions.

Chapter 2
Accounting for Derivatives and Hedges

Introduction

There are two key concepts in the accounting for derivatives and hedges. The first is that ongoing changes in the fair value of derivatives not used in hedging arrangements are generally recognized in earnings at once. The second is that ongoing changes in the fair value of derivatives and the hedged items with which they are paired may be parked in other comprehensive income for a period of time, thereby removing them from the basic earnings reported by a business. In the following sections, we build upon these concepts by addressing the nature of other comprehensive income, the details of the various types of derivative and hedge accounting, and related issues – including controls and disclosures.

Other Comprehensive Income

In the following sections, we will refer to the recordation of certain hedging results in other comprehensive income. What is other comprehensive income?

The intent behind the concept of comprehensive income is to report on all changes in the equity of a business, other than those involving the owners of the business. Not all of these transactions appear in the income statement, so comprehensive income is needed to provide a broader view. Comprehensive income is comprised of net income and other comprehensive income. Other comprehensive income is comprised of the following items:

Foreign Currency Items

- Foreign currency translation adjustments
- Gains and losses on intra-company foreign currency transactions where settlement is not planned in the foreseeable future

Hedging Items

- Gains and losses on derivative instruments that are cash flow hedges
- Gains and losses on foreign currency translation adjustments that are net investment hedges in a foreign entity

Investment Items

- Unrealized holding gains and losses on available-for-sale securities
- Unrealized holding gains and losses resulting from the transfer of a debt security from the held-to-maturity classification to the available-for-sale classification
- Amounts recognized in other comprehensive income for debt securities classified as available-for-sale and held-to-maturity, if the impairment is not recognized in earnings
- Subsequent changes in the fair value of available-for-sale securities that had previously been written down as impaired

Postretirement Benefit Items

- Gains and losses from pension or postretirement benefits that have not been recognized as a component of net periodic benefit cost
- Prior service costs or credits associated with pension or postretirement benefits
- Transition assets or obligations linked to pension or postretirement benefits that have not been recognized as a component of net periodic benefit cost

If the items initially stated in other comprehensive income are later displayed as part of net income (typically because the transactions have been settled), this is essentially a reclassification out of the other comprehensive income classification. Otherwise, the items will be double-counted within comprehensive income. For example, an unrealized gain on an investment is initially recorded within other comprehensive income and is then sold, at which point the gain is realized and shifted from other comprehensive income to net income. In short, there is a continual shifting of items from other comprehensive income to net income over time.

Items of comprehensive income must be reported in a financial statement for the period in which they are recognized. If this information is presented within a single continuous income statement, the presentation encompasses the following:

- Net income and its components
- Other comprehensive income and its components
- Total comprehensive income

EXAMPLE

Armadillo Industries presents the following statement of income and comprehensive income.

Armadillo Industries
Statement of Income and Comprehensive Income
For the Year Ended December 31, 20X2

Revenues		$250,000
Expenses		-200,000
Other gains and losses		10,000
Gain on sale of securities		5,000
Income from operations before tax		$65,000
Income tax expense		-20,000
Net income		$45,000
Other comprehensive income, net of tax		
Foreign currency translation adjustments		2,000
Unrealized holding gains arising during period		11,000
Defined benefit pension plans:		
Prior period service cost arising during period	-$4,000	
Net loss arising during period	-1,000	-5,000
Other comprehensive income		8,000
Comprehensive income, net of tax		$53,000

In addition, the total of other comprehensive income for the reporting period must be stated in the balance sheet in a component of equity that is stated separately from retained earnings and additional paid-in capital.

EXAMPLE

Armadillo Industries reports accumulated other comprehensive income within the equity section of its balance sheet as follows:

Equity:	
Common stock	$1,000,000
Paid-in capital	850,000
Retained earnings	4,200,000
Accumulated other comprehensive income	270,000
Total equity	$6,320,000

Derivative Accounting

The essential accounting for a derivative instrument is outlined in the following bullet points:

- *Initial recognition.* When it is first acquired, recognize a derivative instrument in the balance sheet as an asset or liability at its fair value.
- *Subsequent recognition (hedging relationship).* Recognize all subsequent changes in the fair value of the derivative (known as *marked to market*). If the instrument has been paired with a hedged item, then recognize these fair value changes as noted later in the Presentation of Hedges section.
- *Subsequent recognition (speculation).* Recognize in earnings all subsequent changes in the fair value of the derivative. Speculative activities imply that a derivative has not been paired with a hedged item.

The following additional rules apply to the accounting for derivative instruments when specific types of investments are being hedged:

- *Held-to-maturity investments.* This is a debt instrument for which there is a commitment to hold the investment until its maturity date. When such an investment is being hedged, there may be a change in the fair value of the paired forward contract or purchased option. If so, only recognize a loss in earnings when there is an other-than-temporary decline in the hedging instrument's fair value.
- *Trading securities.* This can be either a debt or equity security, for which there is an intent to sell in the short term for a profit. When this investment is being hedged, recognize any changes in the fair value of the paired forward contract or purchased option in earnings.
- *Available-for-sale securities.* This can be either a debt or equity security that does not fall into the held-to-maturity or trading classifications. When such an investment is being hedged, there may be a change in the fair value of the paired forward contract or purchased option. If so, only recognize a loss in earnings when there is an other-than-temporary decline in the hedging instrument's fair value. If the change is temporary, record it in other comprehensive income.

Hedge Accounting - General

The accounting for hedges involves matching a derivative instrument to a hedged item, and then recognizing gains and losses from both items in the same period. A derivative is always measured at its fair value. If the instrument is effective for a period of time, this may mean that incremental changes in its fair value are continually being recorded in the accounting records.

The intent behind hedge accounting is to allow a business to record changes in the value of a hedging relationship in other comprehensive income (except for fair value hedges), rather than in earnings. This is done in order to protect the core earnings of a business from periodic variations in the value of its financial instruments before they have been liquidated. Once a financial instrument has been liquidated, any accumulated gains or losses stored in other comprehensive income are shifted into earnings.

When a business uses a derivative as a hedge, it can elect to designate the derivative as belonging to one of the following three hedging classifications:

- *Fair value hedge.* The derivative is used to hedge the risk of changes in the fair value of an asset or liability, or of an unrecognized firm commitment.
- *Cash flow hedge.* The derivative is used to hedge variations in the cash flows associated with an asset or liability, or of a forecasted transaction.
- *Foreign currency hedge.* The derivative is used to hedge variations in the foreign currency exposure associated with a net investment in a foreign operation, a forecasted transaction, an available-for-sale security, or an unrecognized firm commitment.

If a derivative instrument is designated as belonging within one of these classifications, the gains or losses associated with the hedge are matched to any gains or losses incurred by the asset or liability with which the derivative is paired. However, the hedging relationship must first qualify for hedge accounting. To do so, the relationship must meet all of the following criteria:

- *Designation.* The hedging relationship must be designated as such at its inception. The documentation of the relationship must include the following:
  - The hedging relationship
  - The risk management objective and strategy, which includes identification of the hedging instrument and the hedged item, the nature of the risk being hedged, and the method used to determine hedge effectiveness.
  - If there is a fair value hedge of a firm commitment, a method for recognizing in earnings the asset or liability that represents the gain or loss on the hedged commitment.
  - If there is a cash flow hedge of a forecasted transaction, the period when the forecasted transaction will occur, the nature of the asset or liability involved, either the amount of foreign exchange being hedged or the number of items encompassed by the transaction, and the current price of the forecasted transaction.

- *Eligibility (hedged item).* Only certain types of assets and liabilities can qualify for special accounting as a hedging relationship.
- *Eligibility (hedging item).* Designate either all or a portion of the hedging instrument as such. Also, several derivative instruments can be jointly designated as the hedging instrument.
- *Effectiveness.* There is an expectation that the pairing will result in a highly effective hedge that offsets prospective changes in the cash flows or fair value associated with the hedged risk. A highly effective hedge is one in which the change in fair value or cash flows of the hedge falls between 80% and 125%

of the opposing change in the fair value or cash flows of the financial instrument that is being hedged. A regression analysis can be used instead of these percentage boundaries to determine hedge effectiveness. Over the life of a hedging relationship, the effectiveness of the pairing must be examined at least quarterly. A prospective analysis should also be made to estimate whether the relationship will be highly effective in future periods, typically using a probability-weighted analysis of changes in fair value or cash flows. If the relationship is no longer highly effective through the date of this assessment, then the pairing no longer qualifies for hedge accounting. It is possible to evaluate a hedging relationship on a qualitative basis if an initial quantitative test was conducted that revealed a highly effective relationship, and there is an expectation of high effectiveness in subsequent periods. If the facts and circumstances supporting a qualitative assessment later change, then conduct a quantitative assessment at that time.

If a hedging relationship is not fully documented or is never documented at all, then all subsequent changes in fair value associated with these instruments must be immediately recorded as gains or losses in earnings.

Even if a hedge is considered to be effective, it is quite possible that some portion of the risk inherent in an underlying transaction will not be covered by a hedge. In this situation, gains and losses on the unhedged portion of a hedged pairing should be recorded in earnings.

EXAMPLE

Suture Corporation pays $1 million for an investment that is denominated in pounds. Suture's treasurer enters into a hedging transaction that is also denominated in pounds, and which is designed to be a hedge of the investment. One year later, Suture experiences a loss of $12,000 on the investment and a $9,000 gain on the hedging instrument. The full $9,000 gain on the hedging instrument is considered effective, so only the difference between the investment and its hedge - $3,000 – is recorded as a loss in earnings.

There may be cases in which a hedging instrument is being employed, where the third party is actually another entity under the umbrella of a parent company. In this case, risk is not being offloaded to a third party. Consequently, such a hedging instrument is not considered to be a hedge for the purposes of hedge accounting.

Hedge Accounting – Fair Value Hedges

The fair value of an asset or liability could change, which may affect the profits of a business. A fair value hedge is designed to hedge against this exposure to changes in fair value that are caused by a specific risk. It is possible to only hedge the risks associated with a portion of an asset or liability, as long as the effectiveness of the related hedge can be measured.

When a hedging relationship has been established for a fair value hedge, continually re-measure the fair value of the hedge and the item with which it is paired. The accounting for this re-measurement is as follows:

- *Hedging item.* Record a gain or loss in earnings for the change in fair value of the hedging instrument.
- *Hedged item.* Record a gain or loss in earnings for the change in fair value of the hedged item that can be attributed to the risk for which the hedge pairing was established. This also means that the carrying amount of the hedged item must be adjusted to reflect its change in fair value.

If the hedging relationship is fully effective, either the gain on the hedging instrument will exactly offset the loss on the hedged item that is associated with the hedged risk, or vice versa. The net result of a fully effective hedge is no change in earnings. If there is a net gain or loss appearing in earnings, it is because the hedging relationship does not perfectly offset fair value changes in the hedged item.

EXAMPLE

Prickly Corporation buys ten bonds having an aggregate face value of $10,000. The bonds pay a 6% interest rate, which matches the current market rate. Prickly records the acquisition as an available-for-sale investment.

Prickly's treasurer reviews the investment, and concludes that an increase in the market rate of interest will reduce the value of the bonds. To hedge this risk, the treasurer enters into an interest rate swap whereby Prickly swaps the fixed 6% interest payments it is receiving from the bond issuer for payments from a third party that are based on a floating interest rate. The treasurer documents the interest rate swap as a hedge of the ten bonds.

Over the following months, the applicable market interest rate does indeed increase, which reduces the value of the bonds by an aggregate amount of $800. However, the interest rate swap yields an offsetting $800 gain, since the variable interest rate payments being received have increased to match the change in the market rate of interest. Prickly first records the following entry to document the loss in value of the bonds:

	Debit	Credit
Hedging loss	800	
Available-for-sale investment (asset)		800

Prickly also records the following entry to document the increased value of the interest rate swap:

	Debit	Credit
Swap asset (asset)	800	
Hedging gain		800

There is no net gain or loss arising from the increase in the market rate of interest, since the loss on the investment is exactly offset by the gain on the hedging instrument. This means the hedge pairing has been 100% effective.

Fair value hedge accounting should be terminated at once if any of the following situations arise:

- The hedging arrangement is no longer effective
- The hedging instrument expires or is sold or terminated
- The organization revokes the hedging designation

As noted in the preceding example, changes in the fair value of the hedged item are being used to adjust its carrying amount over time. Once the item is eventually disposed of, the adjusted carrying amount of the asset is recorded as the cost of the asset sold.

EXAMPLE

The treasurer of Prickly Corporation needs cash for operational requirements, and elects to sell the ten bonds that the company had acquired in the preceding example. In that example, the carrying amount of the bonds had been written down by $800 to reflect an increase in the market interest rate. The bonds are then sold for $9,200, resulting in the following entry:

	Debit	Credit
Cash	9,200	
Available-for-sale investment (asset)		9,200

Hedge Accounting – Cash Flow Hedges

There could be variations in the cash flows associated with an asset or liability or a forecasted transaction, which may affect the profits of a business. A cash flow hedge is designed to hedge against this exposure to changes in cash flows that are caused by a specific risk. It is possible to only hedge the risks associated with a portion of an asset, liability, or forecasted transaction, as long as the effectiveness of the related hedge can be measured. The accounting for a cash flow hedge is as follows:

- *Hedging item.* Include in other comprehensive income the entire change in the fair value of the hedging instrument that was included in the assessment of hedge effectiveness, which are then reclassified to earnings when the hedged item affects earnings.
- *Hedged item.* Initially recognize the effective portion of any gain or loss in other comprehensive income. Reclassify these gains or losses into earnings when the forecasted transaction affects earnings.

There are several additional special situations involving cash flow hedges that require different accounting transactions. The following scenarios reveal the more likely accounting variations:

1. *Exclusions from strategy.* If the documented risk management strategy does not include a certain component of the gains or losses experienced by the hedged item, recognize this excluded amount in earnings. Doing so reduces the aggregate amount of gains or losses in other comprehensive income. Next;

2. *Adjust other comprehensive income.* Reduce the amount of accumulated other comprehensive income related to a hedging relationship to the lesser of:

   - The cumulative gain or loss on the derivative from the date when the hedge began, less any gains or losses already reclassified into earnings; or
   - The cumulative gain or loss on the derivative that will be needed to offset the cumulative change in expected future cash flows on the hedged transaction from the date when the hedge began, less any gains or losses already reclassified into earnings.

3. *Further gain or loss recognition.* Recognize in earnings any remaining gain or loss on the hedging derivative, or to revise the accumulated other comprehensive income amount to match the balance derived in step 2.

4. *Foreign currency adjustments.* If a foreign currency position is being hedged, and hedge effectiveness is based on the total changes in the cash flow of an option, then reclassify from other comprehensive income to earnings an amount sufficient to adjust earnings for the amortization of the option cost.

A key issue with cash flow hedges is when to recognize gains or losses in earnings when the hedging transaction relates to a forecasted transaction. These gains or losses should be reclassified from other comprehensive income to earnings when the hedged transaction affects earnings.

EXAMPLE

Suture Corporation has acquired equipment from a company in the United Kingdom, which Suture must pay for in 60 days in the amount of £150,000. Suture's functional currency is the U.S. Dollar. At the time of the purchase, Suture could settle this obligation for $240,000, based on the exchange rate then in effect.

To hedge against the risk of an unfavorable change in exchange rates during the intervening 60 days, Suture enters into a forward contract with its bank to buy £150,000 in 60 days, at the current exchange rate. Suture's controller designates the forward contract as a hedge of its exposure to adverse changes in the dollar to pounds exchange rate.

At the end of the next month, the pound has increased in value against the dollar, so that it would now require $242,000 to settle the obligation. Luckily, the value of the forward contract has also increased by $2,000, which results in the following entry:

	Debit	Credit
Forward asset (asset)	2,000	
Other comprehensive income		2,000

The exchange rate remains the same for the following month, after which the treasurer settles the forward contract and the controller records the following entry:

	Debit	Credit
Cash (asset)	2,000	
Forward asset (asset)		2,000

The payables staff then pays the $242,000 obligation to the United Kingdom supplier, as noted in the following entry. The transaction also includes a $2,000 reduction of the purchase price, which represents the deferred gain on the forward contract.

	Debit	Credit
Fixed assets – Equipment (asset)	240,000	
Other comprehensive income	2,000	
Cash (asset)		242,000

The net result of this hedging transaction is that Suture has used a hedging instrument to offset the risk of an adverse change in the applicable exchange rate, and so is able to pay for the equipment at the original purchase price.

EXAMPLE

Suture Corporation borrows $10 million on January 1, to be repaid with a balloon payment of $10 million on December 31 of the same year. The interest rate on the loan is SIBOR plus 2.0%, and is to be paid semi-annually. SIBOR on January 1 is 4.50%, so the initial interest rate on the loan is 6.50%. The treasurer of Suture is concerned that interest rates will increase during the borrowing period, and so enters into an interest rate swap with 3rd National Bank on the same day. Under the terms of the swap, Suture pays a fixed interest rate of 6.80% semi-annually for one year, while 3rd National takes over the variable interest payments of Suture. The notional amount of the swap arrangement is $10 million. Suture's cost of capital is 7%.

The swap arrangement qualifies as a cash flow hedge.

On June 30, the interest paid for the first six months of the loan is based on the initial 6.50% interest rate, so Suture records the following entry for a half-year of interest at 6.50% for a $10 million loan:

	Debit	Credit
Interest expense	325,000	
Cash (asset)		325,000

In addition, Suture also pays the net difference in the swapped interest rates of 0.3% on the notional contract amount of $10 million for the same six-month period. The entry is:

	Debit	Credit
Interest expense	15,000	
Cash (asset)		15,000

On June 30, the reference rate adjusts upward to 5.50%, which means that the interest rate on Suture's loan will now be 7.50% for the remaining six months of the loan period. This also means that Suture will be paid the 0.7% difference between the new 7.50% variable interest rate and the 6.80% fixed-rate amount stated in the swap agreement, with this payment being made by 3rd National on the next (and final) payment date, which is December 31. The amount of this payment will be $35,000; when discounted to its present value at Suture's 7% cost of capital for six months, the amount is approximately $33,775. The entry to record this future payment on June 30 is:

	Debit	Credit
Swap contract	33,775	
Other comprehensive income		33,775

On the loan termination date of December 31, Suture makes the following interest expense payment to the lender, based on the 7.50% interest rate that applied to the preceding six-month period:

	Debit	Credit
Interest expense	375,000	
Cash (asset)		375,000

In addition, Suture reverses its accrual of the present value of the swap contract that it recorded on June 30, and replaces it with a recordation of the cash received from 3rd National in settlement of the swap contract. As calculated earlier, the amount of this payment is $35,000.

	Debit	Credit
Other comprehensive income	33,775	
Swap contract		33,775
Cash (asset)	35,000	
Interest expense		35,000

The net undiscounted effect of the interest rate swap is a net decline in Suture's interest expense of $20,000 over the full year covered by the loan, which represents a net decline of 0.2% in the interest rate paid.

Cash flow hedge accounting should be terminated at once if any of the following situations arises:

- The hedging arrangement is no longer effective
- The hedging instrument expires or is terminated
- The organization revokes the hedging designation

If it is probable that the hedged forecasted transaction will not occur within the originally-stated time period or within two months after this period, shift the derivative's gain or loss from accumulated other comprehensive income to earnings.

Hedge Accounting – Net Investment Hedges

A business may have an investment in operations in another country. If so, changes in the exchange rate between the functional currency of the parent entity and the currency of the foreign operations could create gains or losses. In this situation, it is possible to create a net investment hedge that is equal to or less than the carrying amount of the net assets of the foreign operation.

The accounting for such a hedge is to recognize in other comprehensive income the entire change in the fair value of the hedging instrument that was included in the assessment of hedge effectiveness, which is then reclassified to earnings when the hedged item affects earnings. If the parent entity ever disposes of the foreign operations, shift the cumulative net amount of any gains or losses recognized in other comprehensive income as part of the hedging instrument into earnings.

EXAMPLE

Suture Corporation invests $20 million in a new subsidiary located in England. The functional currency of this subsidiary is the pound. The exchange rate on the investment date is $1 = £0.6463, so the initial investment is priced at £12,926,000. Suture takes out a loan in England in the amount of £9,695,000 (which translates to $15,000,000) and designates it as a hedge of its investment in the subsidiary. The stated strategy is that any change in the fair value of the loan attributed to foreign exchange risk will offset 75% of the translation gains or losses on the Suture investment.

One year later, the exchange rate has changed to $1 = £0.6600, which yields the following loss on the investment for Suture:

$$(£12,926,000 \div 0.6600 = \$19,585,000) - \$20,000,000$$

$$= \$(415,000) \text{ Investment translation loss}$$

Against this loss is set the following gain on the related loan:

$$(£9,695,000 \div 0.6600 = \$14,689,000) - \$15,000,000$$

$$= \$311,000 \text{ Loan translation gain}$$

Suture creates the following entry to record the reduction in value of its investment, as well as the translation gain related to its loan:

	Debit	Credit
Cumulative translation adjustment	415,000	
Investment in subsidiary		415,000
Pound-denominated debt	311,000	
Cumulative translation adjustment		311,000

Embedded Derivatives

An embedded derivative is an element of a financial instrument that has the characteristics of a derivative. Thus, the embedded derivative must require that some portion of the cash flows associated with the overall instrument be adjusted in relation to changes in an underlying, as noted earlier. To be an embedded derivative, it is not possible for this element of a financial instrument to be transferred separately from the rest of the contract.

When there is an embedded derivative within a financial instrument, the entire instrument is considered a hybrid financial instrument.

It is possible to separately account for an embedded derivative, but only when both of the following conditions are present:

- The economic characteristics and risks of the derivative element are not closely related to the economic characteristics and risks of the financial instrument in which it is embedded; and
- A separate instrument with the characteristics and risks of the embedded derivative would have been classified as a derivative instrument.

There are several alternatives available for accounting for an embedded derivative, including the following:

- *No separate measurement possible.* If it is not possible to reliably measure an embedded derivative, then measure the entire hybrid financial instrument at its fair value. Also, when there is a change in this fair value, recognize the change in earnings in the reporting period in which the change occurs.
- *Election to combine.* A one-time and irrevocable election can be made to measure the entire hybrid financial instrument at its fair value, with no breakout of the embedded derivative. When there is a change in this fair value, recognize the change in earnings in the reporting period in which the change occurs.
- *Separate accounting.* If the preceding two conditions are present that allow for the separate accounting for an embedded derivative, then the derivative and the contract in which it is embedded are tracked and accounted for separately, based on their respective fair values. However, the sum of their fair values cannot exceed the overall fair value of the hybrid instrument.

EXAMPLE

Hubble Corporation purchases 50 convertible bonds that have been issued by Medusa Medical. Hubble acquires the bonds at face value, so the total amount paid is $50,000. The conversion terms incorporated into the bonds state that each bond contains an option to purchase two shares of Medusa common stock for $14 per share.

The economic characteristics and risks of the option feature are not closely related to the debt features of the bond to which it is attached, and a separate instrument with the option features would have been classified as a derivative instrument. The estimated fair value of the option feature, in aggregate for all 50 bonds, is $600.

Based on this information, Hubble's accountant elects to separately account for the option feature and the bonds. The result is the following initial entry:

	Debit	Credit
Investments (asset)	49,400	
Derivative asset (asset)	600	
Cash (asset)		50,000

Hedging Controls

It is useful to maintain a set of controls designed to ensure that hedging opportunities are properly identified, and that hedges are correctly installed and monitored. The following controls and policies deal with these issues:

- *Match hedge transactions to authorized list.* Have the internal audit staff periodically review all hedging transactions to see if the persons who initiated them were authorized to do so. The auditors should use an approved list of authorized employees as the basis for this analysis.
- *Review transactions prior to completion.* If a company has a history of entering into incorrect hedges, have an in-house hedging specialist review the details of all proposed hedges prior to finalization, to ensure that they are correct and meet the company's hedging objectives.
- *Confirm hedges.* Someone other than the initiator of a hedging transaction should confirm with the counterparty that the hedge is complete, and that both parties agree upon the terms of the hedge. This should involve the physical comparison of the deal terms as stated by both parties.

The following policy is designed to improve the level of control over foreign exchange transactions by centralizing them with a group of (presumably) experienced practitioners:

- *Foreign exchange trading operations shall be centralized at the parent company.* In a highly diverse business, this policy makes it easier to keep track of foreign exchange holdings and forecasted transactions, and to develop appropriate hedges for them.

There are cases where one may be tempted to enter into an over-the-counter hedging transaction with another party, rather than using an exchange. The following policy is designed to limit the number of these over-the-counter transactions:

- *Over-the-counter hedges must be approved in advance by the CFO.* There is a risk that the counterparty in an over-the-counter transaction will not fulfill its obligations under a hedge, resulting in a loss for the company. This policy is designed to limit the number of such transactions.

A policy that can be of use where there are large foreign exchange positions is a requirement to periodically stress-test a company's hedging strategy, as shown below:

- *The company's foreign exchange hedging strategy shall be stress-tested at least quarterly to determine losses under various hedging scenarios.* This policy mandates that the treasury staff periodically create a stress model that calculates the company's worst-case losses, based on its existing hedging strategy. The concept can be expanded further, to incorporate alternative hedging strategies and their projected results. The outcome of this analysis may be adjustments to the corporate hedging strategy to mitigate possible losses.

The following policy can be of use in providing specific guidance in regard to the amount of hedging can be engaged in:

- *The benchmark hedge ratio shall be no less than __% for booked exposures and __% for forecasted exposures.* This ratio is the proportion of the dollar volume of certain transactions that will be hedged. This policy sets specific hedging targets, which may be close to 100% for booked exposures and considerably less for forecasted exposures. The forecasted exposure target is lower, since it is difficult to estimate the amount of these more distant cash flows.

Sample Hedging Procedure

When a business has current or expected holdings or obligations involving foreign currencies, it may be prudent to create a hedging transaction to mitigate the company's potential losses arising from exchange rate fluctuations. A foreign exchange hedging procedure is outlined below:

1. **Calculate hedge requirements.** Based on the company's forecast of foreign currency holdings or obligations, determine the amount and duration of the hedging transaction needed to offset these holdings or obligations.
   Responsible party: Treasury staff

2. **Examine preliminary hedge.** Obtain information about the prospective hedge, and address the following issues:
   - Verify the sufficiency of the counterparty's credit rating
   - Determine the level of effectiveness of the hedging strategy
   - Review the proposed contract for legal issues
   - Obtain approval of the hedge

   Responsible party: Treasury staff, treasurer, and corporate counsel
   Control issues: It may be useful to use a proposed hedge signoff sheet, so that each person involved in a hedge can formally document that their assigned tasks were completed.

3. **Begin hedge.** Enter into the hedging transaction.
   Responsible party: Treasury staff
   Control issues: Be sure to confirm the details of the hedging transaction with the counterparty. Otherwise, you may find that the terms of the hedge do not meet the company's expectations, and may need to close out the transaction and start over.

4. **Document the hedge.** Create all hedging documentation required under the applicable accounting standards. This includes documentation of:
   - How the company plans to measure the effectiveness of the hedging transaction

- The relationship between the foreign exchange position and the hedging instrument
- The risk management objectives of the company
- The specifics of the hedging strategy

This information is needed to properly account for the hedge.

Responsible party: Treasury staff

Control issues: Be sure to confirm the details of the hedging transaction with the counterparty. Otherwise, you may find that the terms of the hedge do not meet the company's expectations.

5. **Account for the hedge.** At the end of each reporting period, charge to other comprehensive income any gains or losses resulting from having marked the hedge to market. If any hedge losses are considered to be non-recoverable and they have previously been recorded in other comprehensive income, shift them to earnings.

   Responsible party: Accounting staff

   Control issues: To ensure that this step is completed, include it in the list of period-end closing activities.

6. **Close out the hedge.** Once the hedging transaction has been completed and settled, move all gains and losses initially recorded in the other comprehensive income account to earnings.

   Responsible party: Accounting staff

   Control issues: Review the other comprehensive income account to ensure that all transactions related to a closed hedge have been removed from that account.

The following exhibit shows a streamlined view of the foreign exchange hedging procedure.

Foreign Exchange Hedging Process Flow

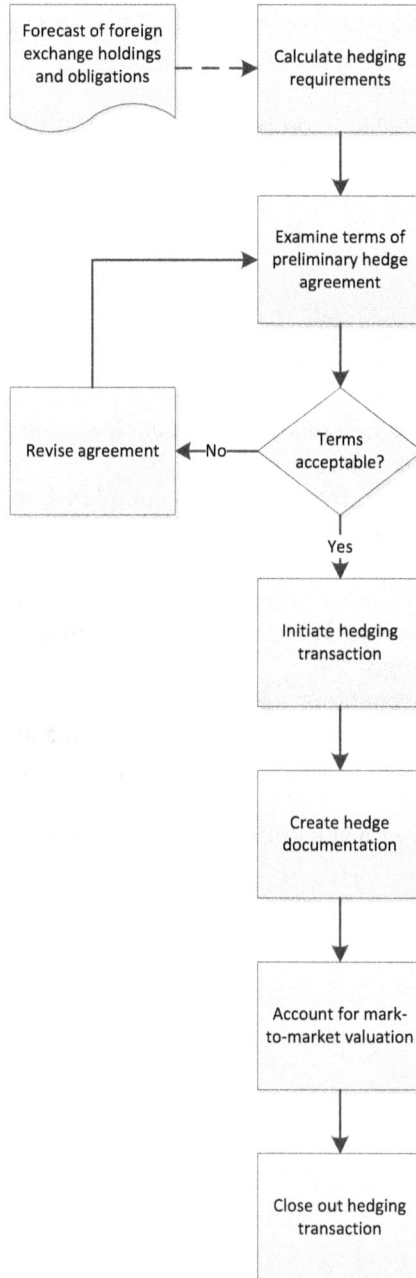

```
Forecast of foreign          Calculate hedging
exchange holdings    ----->   requirements
and obligations

                              Examine terms of
                     ----->   preliminary hedge
                    |         agreement
                    |
                    |              |
                    |              v
  Revise agreement  <--No--   Terms
                              acceptable?

                                  | Yes
                                  v

                              Initiate hedging
                              transaction

                                  |
                                  v

                              Create hedge
                              documentation

                                  |
                                  v

                              Account for mark-
                              to-market valuation

                                  |
                                  v

                              Close out hedging
                              transaction
```

The sample procedure shown in this section could be expanded upon to deal with other types of hedging transactions.

Unhedged Foreign Exchange Gains and Losses

There may be circumstances when a choice is made not to create a hedge against a foreign exchange position, and the company subsequently incurs a gain or loss on that position. It is also possible that the company does not have an adequate foreign exchange forecasting system, and so does not know that it even has unhedged positions, which will most certainly result in unhedged gains or losses.

In either case, it is extremely useful to keep track of gains or losses arising from unhedged foreign currency positions, in order to estimate when the size of these gains or losses warrants the imposition of a more extensive hedging program. The simplest form of metric is a trend line analysis. This trend line will likely yield results that routinely bounce between gains and losses. The key issue to watch for is an increasing trend in the *size* of the gains or losses over time. When they become large enough to seriously impact the company's reported results from operations, it is time to consider a combination of a better forecasting system and a more active hedging program.

Presentation of Hedges

An organization should present the earnings effect of its hedging instruments in the same income statement line item in which the earnings effect of the hedged item is being reported. This includes the following:

- *Fair value hedges*. Include in earnings the entire change in the fair value of the hedging instrument that was included in the assessment of hedge effectiveness.
- *Cash flow hedges*. Include in other comprehensive income the entire change in the fair value of the hedging instrument that was included in the assessment of hedge effectiveness, which are then reclassified to earnings when the hedged item affects earnings.
- *Net investment hedges*. Include in the currency translation adjustment section of other comprehensive income the entire change in the fair value of the hedging instrument that was included in the assessment of hedge effectiveness, which is then reclassified to earnings when the hedged item affects earnings.

Derivative and Hedging Disclosures

There are a number of specific disclosures related to derivatives and hedging, as well as more specific disclosure requirements for fair value hedges, cash flow hedges, and net investment hedges. In the following sub-sections, we address the disclosures required for each of these areas. Please note that all quantitative disclosures should be presented in a tabular format.

General Disclosures

The following information should be disclosed about the derivative positions and hedging activities of a business in the notes that accompany its financial statements;

the disclosures should be made separately for cash flow hedging instruments, fair value hedging instruments, foreign currency hedging instruments, and all other derivatives:

- *Overview*. The objectives and strategies of the entity's derivatives program, including how and why the business uses them. This information can be more meaningful to the reader if the discussion is in the context of overall risk exposures relating to risks for interest rates, foreign exchange, commodity prices, credit, and equity prices.
- *Accounting*. How the derivatives and hedged items are accounted for by the organization.
- *Impact*. The effect of the hedging activities on the financial position, financial results, and cash flows of the business.
- *Totals*. The total amount of each income and expense line item appearing in the income statement in which the results of fair value or cash flow hedges are recorded.
- *Volume*. The volume of activity in the organization's derivatives program.

In addition, the business should separately present, by type of contract, any gains and losses on derivative instruments that were not designated as or qualifying as hedging instruments.

SAMPLE DISCLOSURE

As a matter of policy, we use derivatives for risk management purposes, and we do not use derivatives for speculative purposes. A key risk management objective for our leasing business is to mitigate interest rate and currency risk by seeking to ensure that the characteristics of the debt match the assets they are funding. If the form (fixed versus floating) and currency denomination of the debt we issue do not match the related assets, we typically execute derivatives to adjust the nature and tenor of funding to meet this objective within pre-defined limits. The determination of whether we enter into a derivative transaction or issue debt directly to achieve this objective depends on a number of factors, including market-related factors that affect the type of debt we can issue.

The notional amounts of derivative contracts represent the basis upon which interest and other payments are calculated and are reported gross, except for offsetting foreign currency forward contracts that are executed in order to manage our currency risk of net investment in foreign subsidiaries. Of the outstanding notional amount of $40 million, approximately 87%, or $28 million, is associated with reducing or eliminating the interest rate, currency or market risk between financial assets and liabilities in our leasing business. The remaining derivative activities primarily relate to hedging against adverse changes in currency exchange rates related to anticipated sales and purchases and contracts containing certain clauses that meet the accounting definition of a derivative. The instruments used in these activities are designated as hedges when practicable.

In addition, the following information should be disclosed by contract type:

- *Fair values.* The fair values of all derivatives recognized in the balance sheet, as well as the line items in which they are located.
- *Fair value hedge totals.* The gains or losses on derivatives and the hedged items with which they are paired for fair value hedges.
- *Cash flow hedge totals.* The gains or losses on derivatives and the hedged items with which they are paired for cash flow hedges.
- *All other hedge totals.* The gains or losses on derivatives and the hedged items with which they are paired for all other hedges.

SAMPLE DISCLOSURE

Fair Value of Derivative Instruments at December 31, 20X5:

(000s)	Derivative Assets		Derivative Liabilities	
	Balance Sheet Location	Fair Value	Balance Sheet Location	Fair Value
Hedging Instruments				
Interest rate contracts	Other assets	$13,000	Other liabilities	-$7,000
Foreign exchange contracts	Other assets	27,000	Other liabilities	-12,000
Commodity contracts	Other assets	3,000	Other liabilities	-2,000
Totals		$43,000		-$21,000
Non-Hedging Instruments				
Interest rate contracts	Other assets	$3,000	Other liabilities	-$2,000
Foreign exchange contracts	Other assets	9,000	Other liabilities	-4,000
Commodity contracts	Other assets	2,000	Other liabilities	-1,000
Total		$14,000		-$7,000
Total derivatives		$57,000		-$28,000

If there are disclosures related to derivatives in several footnotes, cross-reference the information across the footnotes.

Fair Value Hedge Disclosures

The following additional disclosures should be made when the organization engages in fair value hedging transactions:

- *Exclusions from hedge effectiveness.* State any portion of the gains and losses on any portion of derivative instruments that were excluded from the assessment of hedge effectiveness and recognized in earnings.

- *Terminated qualification.* When a hedged firm commitment no longer qualifies as a fair value hedge, note the net gain or loss that was recognized in earnings.
- *Tabular presentation.* Disclose the following items in a tabular format for items designated and qualifying as hedged items in fair value hedges:
  - The carrying amount of hedged assets and liabilities reported in the balance sheet;
  - The cumulative amount of fair value hedging adjustments relating to these hedged assets and liabilities;
  - The balance sheet line item that includes these hedged assets and liabilities; and
  - The cumulative amount of any remaining fair value hedging adjustments for hedged assets and liabilities where hedge accounting has been discontinued.

Cash Flow Hedge Disclosures

The following additional disclosures should be made when the organization engages in cash flow hedging transactions:

- *Reclassifications.* The transactions that caused a reclassification of gains or losses from other comprehensive income to earnings.
- *Estimated reclassifications.* The estimated amount of gains or losses that are expected to be reclassified from other comprehensive income to earnings within the next 12 months.
- *Exposure duration.* The maximum period over which the organization is hedging its exposure to the future cash flows arising from forecasted transactions.
- *Discontinuance reclassifications.* The amount of the gains or losses that were reclassified from other comprehensive income to earnings, due to cash flow hedges being discontinued because it is no longer probable that forecasted transactions will occur during the planned time period.
- *Gains and losses.* Any gains and losses on derivative instruments that were associated with cash flow hedges and included in the assessment of hedge effectiveness, that were recognized within other comprehensive income within the period. Also disclose the amounts that were reclassified into earnings during the current period.
- *Exclusions from hedge effectiveness.* State any portion of the gains and losses on any portion of derivative instruments that were excluded from the assessment of hedge effectiveness and recognized in earnings.
- *Net changes.* The beginning and ending accumulated gain or loss for derivatives, including for the current period the net changes caused by current period hedging activities and the net amount of all reclassifications into earnings.

In addition, note in a separate line item within the statement of comprehensive income the net gain or loss on derivative instruments that have been designated as cash flow hedges.

SAMPLE DISCLOSURE

For derivatives that are designated in a cash flow hedging relationship, the effective portion of the change in fair value of the derivative is reported as a component of other comprehensive income and reclassified into earnings contemporaneously and in the same caption with the earnings effects of the hedged transaction.

We expect to transfer $28 million to earnings as an expense in the next 12 months contemporaneously with the earnings effects of the related forecasted transactions.

At December 31, 20X3 and 20X2, the maximum term of derivative instruments that hedge forecasted transactions was 9 years and 10 years, respectively.

In 20X3, we recognized insignificant gains and losses related to hedged forecasted transactions and firm commitments that did not occur by the end of the originally specified period.

The following table provides information about the amounts recorded in other comprehensive income, as well as the gain (loss) recorded in earnings, when reclassified out of other comprehensive income, for the years ended December 31, 20X3 and 20X2, respectively.

(000s)	Gain (Loss) Recognized in Accumulated Other Comprehensive Income		Gain (Loss) Reclassified from Accumulated Other Comprehensive Income into Earnings	
	20X7	20X6	20X7	20X6
Interest rate contracts	-$114	-$73	-$342	-$210
Currency exchange contracts	582	389	436	291
Totals	$468	$316	$94	$81

SAMPLE DISCLOSURE

	Location and Amounts of Gain or Loss Recognized in Income on Fair Value and Cash Flow Hedging Relationships					
	20X4			20X3		
	Revenue	Cost of Goods Sold	Interest Income (Expense)	Revenue	Cost of Goods Sold	Interest Income (Expense)
Total amounts of income and expense line items presented in the balance sheet in which the effects of fair value or cash flow hedges are recorded	$1,850,000	$128,000	$42,000	$930,000	$283,000	$20,000
Gain (or loss) on fair value hedging relationships						
Interest contracts:						
Hedged items			10,000			3,000
Derivatives designated as hedged items			32,000			17,000
Foreign exchange contracts:						
Hedged items	720,000			610,000		
Derivatives designated as hedging instruments	1,130,000			320,000		
Commodity contracts:						
Amount of gain reclassified from accumulated other comprehensive income into income		98,000			233,000	
Amount excluded from effectiveness testing recognized in earnings based on changes in fair value		30,000			50,000	

Net Investment Hedge Disclosures

If an organization has a net investment hedge, it should present gains and losses separately for each of the following, by type of contract:

- *Current gains and losses.* State all gains and losses on both derivative and non-derivative instruments that were designated and qualified as net investment hedges, and that were recognized in the current period within the cumulative translation adjustment section of other comprehensive income.
- *Prior gains and losses.* State all gains and losses over the term of the hedging relationship on both derivative and non-derivative instruments that were designated and qualified as net investment hedges, which were reclassified into earnings during the current period.

- *Excluded gains and losses*. State all gains and losses on both derivative and non-derivative instruments that were designated and qualified as net investment hedges, which were excluded from the assessment of hedge effectiveness.

Summary

The accounting for derivatives and hedges is among the most complex in all of accounting, especially for outlier situations where the circumstances must be closely examined to ensure that the proper accounting rules are followed. In many instances, and especially when the accountant is dealing with a new transaction, it can make sense to consult with the company's auditors regarding the proper accounting to use.

The payoff for this high level of accounting complexity is a delay in the recognition of gains or losses in earnings. If management is not concerned about more immediate recognition, or if the gains or losses are minor, it may make sense to ignore the multitude of compliance issues associated with hedge accounting. Instead, simply create hedges as needed and record gains or losses on foreign exchange holdings and hedges at once, without worrying about the proper documentation of each hedging relationship and having to repeatedly measure hedge effectiveness.

Glossary

A

Available-for-sale securities. Investments that are not classified as held-to-maturity or trading securities.

C

Carrying amount. The recorded amount of an asset, net of any accumulated depreciation or accumulated impairment losses.

Comprehensive income. The change in equity of a business during a period, not including investments by or distributions to owners.

Credit default swap. A contract that transfers credit exposure between parties.

Credit rating. A published score relating to an entity's ability to repay a debt obligation.

Credit risk. The risk that a borrower will not pay back a loan, or that the counterparty to a contract will not pay.

D

Derivative financial instrument. A financial contract whose value depends on the price of an underlying asset or benchmark.

F

Fair value. The price paid for an asset or liability in an orderly transaction between market participants.

Fair value hedge. A hedge of the exposure to changes in the fair value of an asset or liability that is attributable to a specific risk.

Financial instrument. A document that has monetary value or which establishes an obligation to pay.

Financial risk. The risk that changes in the markets will have a negative impact on the profits of a business.

Forecasted transaction. A transaction that is expected to occur at a later date, but for which there is no firm commitment.

Foreign currency. A currency other than the functional currency being used by an entity.

Foreign exchange rate. The price at which one currency can be converted into a different currency.

Foreign exchange risk. The risk that the value of an investment will be reduced by changes in the applicable foreign exchange rate.

Forward rate agreement (FRA). An agreement between two parties to lock in a specific interest rate for a designated period of time.

Futures contract. A standardized agreement to buy or sell a financial instrument at a specific price and on a specific date, which can be traded on an exchange.

H

Hedge. An action taken to reduce an existing or expected risk.

Held-to-maturity securities. A debt security that the holder intends to hold to maturity, and who has the ability to do so.

I

Interest rate. The rate charged for the use of money for a period of time.

Interest rate risk. The risk that changes in interest rates will have a negative effect on an entity's profits.

Interest rate swap. An agreement to swap the future cash flows related to interest payments.

N

Net income. Revenues and gains, less expenses and losses, not including items of other comprehensive income.

Notional amount. The face value of a financial instrument, which is used to make calculations based on that amount.

O

Option. A contract that gives the holder the right, but not the obligation, to purchase or sell an asset at a specific price for a designated period of time.

Other comprehensive income. Revenue, expense, gain, and loss items that are excluded from net income but included in comprehensive income.

S

Security. An interest in an entity or an obligation of the issuer that is represented by an instrument that is a medium of investment, and which is divisible into a class of shares or other interests.

Swap. An arrangement to engage in an exchange, usually related to cash payment obligations.

Swaption. An option on a swap arrangement, giving the holder the right, but not the obligation, to enter into a swap arrangement or alter the terms of a swap.

T

Trading securities. Securities acquired with the intent of selling them in the near term to generate a profit.

U

Underlying. A variable, such as an interest rate, exchange rate, or commodity price, that is used to determine the settlement of a derivative instrument.

Unrealized gain or loss. The difference between the carrying amount and market price of a financial instrument that has not yet been sold.

Index

www.ingramcontent.com/pod-product-compliance
Lightning Source LLC
Chambersburg PA
CBHW051423200326
41520CB00023B/7337